Fondue

AND TABLE TOP COOKERY

SWISS FONDUE *(Photograph: Swiss Cheese Union)*

Fondue

AND TABLE TOP COOKERY

By Marion Howells

Octopus Books – Angus & Robertson

Contents

Fondues

Table Top Cookery

This edition first published 1971 by
Octopus Books Limited
67 Fleet Street, London EC 4

© 1971 Octopus Books Ltd

Distributed in Australia by
Angus & Robertson (Publishers) Pty Ltd
102 Glover Street, Cremorne Sydney

ISBN 7064 0011 9
Printed in Hong Kong

Introduction

This is essentially a book for entertaining and entertaining of the more intimate type.
A Fondue party can be great fun – but limit the numbers to five or six. If you prepare as much as possible beforehand, you can relax and your guests will enjoy the informal atmosphere.

Fondues

This popular dish originated in Switzerland. Many stories are told of the villagers being isolated in the long winter months, and supplies of food becoming short, they were forced to rely on local produce like cheese, wine and home made bread. As the cheese became dry they melted it in their wine. Be that as it may – the word fondue, from the French 'fondre' means to melt or blend and a fondue is basically cheese melted in wine. Originally, a thick earthenware pan, called a 'caquelon' was used to make the fondue, so that the cheese melted slowly and did not become stringy. But modern fondue pots, in addition to the earthenware ones, can be made of copper, stainless steel or a combination of both, or vitrified cast iron, particularly suitable for Fondue Bourguignonne which will be discussed later. All are very attractive. You will also need a spirit lamp with an adjustable flame and special fondue forks which have long handles. Many manufacturers, of course, sell the complete fondue set.
The different cantons of Switzerland have their own special versions of fondue, but generally a mixture of Emmenthal and Gruyère cheese is used. In the recipes which follow you will find various other kinds used including Cheddar, but as the fat content is rather lower than in some of the Swiss cheeses it may be necessary to add a small nut of butter to prevent the fondue sticking.
A touch of garlic is traditional – but this may always be omitted. The cheese is melted slowly in the wine, and a little lemon juice is added as

7

the acidity helps to melt the cheese. Also traditional is the addition of Kirsch. This is mixed with a little cornflour (cornstarch) to help in the thickening.

Choose a dry white wine. It need not be expensive; a Riesling or Hock is a good choice and the same wine can be served during the meal or while the fondue is being prepared, although very often the Swiss drink tea with their fondue.

This is not a dish for a hurried meal – the cheese should be melted slowly, and if it is a cold dark night with the curtains drawn, and perhaps by candlelight, your guests will sit round happily chatting – possibly reminiscing about Fondue parties during a skiing holiday.

If, by any chance, the fondue should curdle, a few drops of lemon juice and a vigorous beat will put it right.

If you feel it is too thick, add a little more warm wine and if it seems thin, add a little more cornflour (cornstarch) but don't forget to blend it with a little Kirsch or wine before stirring it into the fondue.

Provide fondue forks and plenty of French bread. The idea is to spear a piece of bread onto the fork and dip it into the fondue. The bread should not be so fresh that it crumbles in the fondue and it is best to leave the crust on as it is easier to spear on to the fork.

Fondue parties are becoming increasingly popular with people of all ages. The minimum amount of preparation is required, there is little washing up afterwards and it is fun for both the host and the guests. A system of forteits adds to the excitement – If a man drops his bread in the fondue he buys a bottle of wine, and if a lady drops hers, she must kiss all the men at the table. Fondue is served as the main course, often accompanied by a green salad and then followed with fresh fruit or, if the season is right, an open cherry tart or flan.

Among the recipes which follow will be found some for quite substantial fondues.

8

Cheese
Fondues

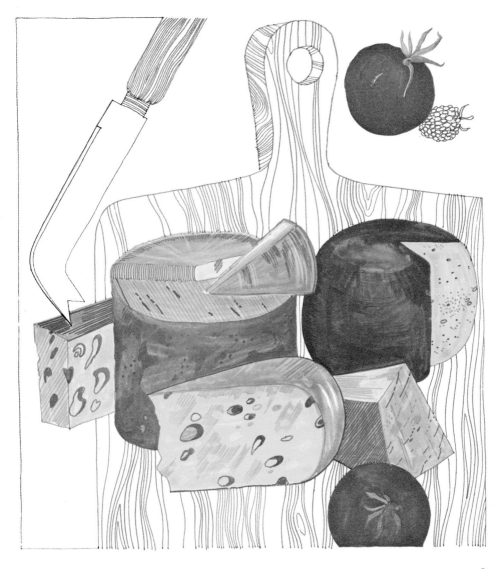

Swiss Fondue

This recipe is for the traditional Neuchatel Fondue. In the following pages you will find many variations.

1 clove garlic
¾ pint (1½ cups) dry white wine
1 teaspoon lemon juice
white pepper, cayenne pepper, grated nutmeg, paprika

¾ lb. (3 cups) grated Emmenthal cheese
¾ lb. (3 cups) grated Gruyère cheese
2 teaspoons cornflour (cornstarch)
3 tablespoons Kirsch

Rub the inside of the fondue pot with garlic. Put in the wine and lemon juice and heat over a low flame. Add the cheese gradually, stirring all the time using a figure of eight motion. When the mixture bubbles, add the cornflour blended smoothly with the Kirsch and cook for about 3 minutes. Add pepper, cayenne, nutmeg and paprika to taste.
Serves 4

Cheese Fondue

In the recipe for Swiss Fondue above a mixture of Gruyère and Emmenthal cheese is used. In this recipe only one kind is needed.

1 clove of garlic
2 wineglasses dry white wine
1 lb. (4 cups) grated Gruyère cheese

1 teaspoon arrowroot
1 liqueur glass of Kirsch
1 tablespoon butter

Rub the inside of the fondue pot with the cut garlic.
Add the wine, heat for a minute then add the cheese.
Stir continuously over medium heat until the fondue thickens.
Mix the arrowroot smoothly with the Kirsch and stir into the mixture. Add the butter and stir until it has melted.
The fondue is then ready for use.
Serves 3-4

Simple Tomato Fondue

1 clove garlic
3 tablespoons butter
4 tomatoes, peeled, seeded
   and chopped
1 teaspoon dried sweet basil
$\frac{1}{2}$ teaspoon oregano

$\frac{1}{2}$ teaspoon paprika
1 glass dry white wine
1 lb. (4 cups) grated Cheddar
   cheese
French bread

Rub the inside of the fondue pot with the cut garlic. Put in the butter and when it has melted add the tomatoes, basil and oregano. Cook for 6-8 minutes then add paprika and wine. Heat, then gradually add the cheese and stir over low heat until it has melted and the mixture is thick and creamy. Check the seasoning – a little salt may be required but it depends on the cheese.
Serves 3-4

Fondue with Mushrooms

1 lb. button mushrooms
4 oz. ($\frac{1}{2}$ cup) butter
1 clove of garlic
1 lb. (4 cups) grated Gruyère
   cheese

$\frac{1}{4}$ pint ($\frac{1}{2}$ cup) dry white wine
1 teaspoon cornflour
   (cornstarch)
1 glass Kirsch

Preparation
Wipe the mushrooms and sauté them in about $\frac{3}{4}$ of the butter.

At the table
Rub the fondue pot with the cut clove of garlic. Put in the wine, heat a little, then add the cheese and stir over gentle heat until the fondue thickens. Add the cornflour mixed smoothly with the Kirsch and the remaining butter.
Allow to bubble for a few minutes when it will be ready for your guests to spear their mushrooms and dip them in the fondue. Provide some cubes or slices of French bread as well.
Serves 3-4

Cheese Fondue with Eggs

6 eggs
4 oz. ($\frac{1}{2}$ cup) butter
4 oz. (1 cup) grated Gruyère
  cheese
4 oz. (1 cup) grated Cheddar
  cheese

2 oz. ($\frac{1}{2}$ cup) grated Parmesan
  cheese
4 tablespoons dry white wine
salt, pepper

Beat the eggs and put them into the fondue pot over very low heat. When they are just beginning to set, stir in the butter in small pieces. When it has all been added, stir in the cheese and wine. Season and continue to stir over low heat until the fondue is thick and creamy.

Your guests should be all ready with their fondue forks and French bread as this fondue is best if not left in the pot too long.

Serves 3-4

Fondue with Herbs

1 clove garlic
$\frac{1}{4}$ pint ($\frac{1}{2}$ cup) dry white
  wine
1 lb. ($3\frac{1}{2}$ cups) Gouda cheese,
  grated
3 teaspoons cornflour
  (cornstarch)

2 tablespoons Kirsch
1 teaspoon finely chopped
  parsley
$\frac{1}{2}$ teaspoon finely chopped
  tarragon
pinch of black pepper
pinch of nutmeg

Rub the inside of the fondue pot with the cut garlic.
Put in the wine, heat a little then add the cheese gradually and stir until it has melted and the mixture begins to bubble.
Add the cornflour, blended smoothly with the kirsch, parsley, tarragon, black pepper and nutmeg. Allow it to bubble for a minute or so and the fondue is ready.
Have slices of French bread ready and a green salad would be a good accompaniment.

Serves 4

FONDUE WITH HERBS (Photograph · The Dutch Dairy Bureau)

English Style Fondue

$\frac{1}{2}$ pint (1 cup) ale or beer
$\frac{1}{2}$ lb. (2 cups) grated Cheddar
   cheese
1 clove garlic, crushed
little extra ale

2 tablespoons butter
$\frac{1}{2}$ teaspoon dry mustard
2 tablespoons cornflour
   (cornstarch)

Put the beer, cheese and crushed garlic into the fondue pot
and stir over low heat until the cheese has melted.
Stir in the butter. Mix the mustard and cornflour smoothly
with a little extra beer and stir into the fondue. Stir until the
mixture is thick and creamy.
Serves 3-4

Geneva Fondue

*This is a rich thin fondue generally eaten with noodles. Have them cooked
and kept hot while the fondue is being made.*

8 egg yolks
$\frac{1}{2}$ lb. (2 cups) grated Gruyère
   cheese
little grated nutmeg

salt, pepper
4 oz. ($\frac{1}{2}$ cup) butter
$\frac{1}{4}$ pint double (heavy) cream

Beat the egg yolks and put into the fondue pot with the
cheese, nutmeg and pepper and salt to taste.
When the cheese has melted, add the butter a little at a time
and stirring continuously over gentle heat.
When the mixture thickens, add the cream. Stir for a few
minutes longer then pour over the noodles.
Serves 3-4

Bernese Fondue

This fondue generally contains a mixture of cheeses including Sbrinz, probably the oldest Swiss hard cheese, from the South Central Alps region. It is not generally exported and the Sprinz cheese sold in America comes from Argentina and is really a variety of Parmesan.

1 clove garlic
2 oz. ($\frac{1}{2}$ stick) butter
2-3 shallots, peeled
2 oz. (1 cup) button
   mushrooms
$\frac{1}{2}$ bottle dry white wine
$\frac{3}{4}$ lb. (3 cups) grated
   Emmenthal cheese
$\frac{3}{4}$ lb. (3 cups) grated Gruyère
   cheese

2 oz. ($\frac{1}{2}$ cup) grated Parmesan
   or Sprinz cheese
$\frac{1}{4}$ teaspoon each dry mustard,
   paprika and grated nutmeg
2 tablespoons sherry
3 teaspoons cornflour
   (cornstarch)
French bread

Rub the cut clove of garlic round the inside of the fondue pot. Add the butter and when it has melted add the shallots and mushrooms. Cook for 5-10 minutes.
Stir in the white wine and when hot, but not boiling, add the cheeses and stir continuously until melted. Add seasoning.
Add the cornflour blended smoothly with the sherry. Stir until almost boiling then simmer for about 15 minutes stirring all the time in the form of a figure of eight. It should now be ready for use.
Serves 4-5

Fondue Italienne

One of the Italian cheeses, Pecorino or Provolone, should be used in this fondue. All the various kinds of Pecorino cheese are made from ewe's milk and a great deal is exported. Provolone cheese comes in a variety of shapes and has a strong flavour. If neither is available, use Parmesan.

1 clove garlic
$\frac{1}{2}$ pint (1 cup) dry white wine
1 teaspoon lemon juice
1 lb. (4 cups) grated Cheddar
   cheese
$\frac{1}{4}$ lb. (1 cup) grated Provolone,
   Pecorino or Parmesan
   cheese

2 tablespoons cornflour
   (cornstarch)
4 tablespoons Kirsch or sherry
French bread

Rub the inside of the fondue pot with the cut clove of garlic. Add the wine and lemon juice and warm over low heat. Add the cheese gradually and stir until it has melted, keeping the heat low. Mix the cornflour smoothly with the Kirsch, add to the cheese mixture and stir until the fondue bubbles and is thick and creamy.

Serves 4-5

Buffet Fondue

This is ideal for a buffet party. The fondue can be left over a very low heat and guests can help themselves as they wish.
Prepare a tray of suitable foods – cocktail sausages, prawns, mushrooms previously sautéd in a little butter, diced aubergine (egg plant), small flowerets of cauliflower, stuffed olives, cubes of ham etc. and of course, plenty of cubed French bread.

For the Fondue

1 clove garlic
$\frac{3}{4}$ pint ($1\frac{1}{2}$ cups) dry white wine
1 teaspoon lemon juice
$\frac{3}{4}$ lb. (3 cups) grated Gruyère cheese

$\frac{3}{4}$ lb. (3 cups) grated Cheddar cheese
1 tablespoon cornflour (cornstarch)
3 tablespoons Kirsch
white pepper, grated nutmeg, paprika

Rub round the inside of the fondue pot with the cut clove of garlic. Add the wine and lemon juice, heat for a few minutes then gradually add the cheese stirring continuously until the mixture bubbles.

Mix the cornflour smoothly with the Kirsch, stir into the fondue and cook another 3-4 minutes. Add pepper, nutmeg and paprika to taste.

Keep the fondue hot over very low heat and see that it is stirred from time to time.

Serves 4-5

Chamois Cheese Fondue

A packet of Chamois Cheese Fondue

Method
Empty contents into a flame-proof dish or pan and prepare as directed. To serve, transfer into a traditional fondue dish to keep the cheese hot. Dip cubes of crusty French bread into the bubbling fondue. Accompany with a fairly dry white wine such as Neuchatel or a Riesling.
Alternatively, hot tea may be served.

Fondue Anchois

1 tablespoon butter
$\frac{1}{2}$ lb. (2 cups) grated Cheddar
   cheese
2 teaspoons cornflour
   (cornstarch)
5 tablespoons warm milk
1 teaspoon Worcestershire
   sauce

2 teaspoons anchovy essence
white pepper
$\frac{1}{2}$ teaspoon paprika
1 egg, separated
2 tablespoons sherry
French bread cut into cubes

Put the butter and grated cheese into the fondue pot and stir over very low heat until the cheese has melted.
Mix the cornflour smoothly with the warm milk, stir into the melted cheese and add the Worcestershire sauce, anchovy essence, a dash of white pepper and paprika.
Stir continuously until the mixture thickens. Add the beaten egg yolk and cook a further minute without boiling.
Remove from the heat, add the sherry and stir in the stiffly beaten egg white.
Serves 2-3

Dutch Fondue

*Many years ago, the farmers' wives in Holland used their cheeses which
were not perfect in shape for making fondue.*
*Dutch gin was generally used for flavouring, but in this recipe, Kirsch,
Whisky, Brandy or Sherry could be used.*

14 oz. ($3\frac{1}{2}$ cups) Gouda or
    Edam cheese, grated
$\frac{1}{2}$ clove garlic
$\frac{1}{4}$ pint ($\frac{1}{2}$ cup) dry white wine
1 teaspoon lemon juice

1 tablespoon cornflour
    (cornstarch)
$1\frac{1}{2}$ tablespoons Dutch gin
freshly ground black pepper,
    pinch nutmg

Rub the inside of the pan with the cut garlic. Put in the wine
and lemon juice and heat slowly until the wine is nearly
boiling. Add the cheese a little at a time stirring continuously
with a fork, until all the cheese has melted.
Blend the cornflour smoothly with the gin and when the
mixture boils, stir in the blended cornflour.
Add a dash of black pepper and the nutmeg.
Have cubes of French bread ready and if liked, a tossed green
salad.
Serves 4

Tomato Fondue with Frankfurters

1 clove garlic
$\frac{1}{2}$ lb. (2 cups) grated Cheddar cheese
2 oz. ($\frac{1}{2}$ cup) grated Gruyère cheese
1 teaspoon Worcestershire sauce
$\frac{1}{4}$ pint ($\frac{1}{2}$ cup) condensed tomato soup
3 tablespoons sherry
1 small can cocktail frankfurter sausages
French bread

Rub the inside of the fondue pot with the cut garlic.
Put in the cheese, tomato soup and Worcestershire sauce and stir continuously over low heat until the cheese has melted, and the mixture is creamy.
Stir in the sherry and cook a further 2-3 minutes.
Check the seasoning before serving.
The cocktail sausages are then speared on the fondue forks and dipped into the fondue.
Serve with plenty of French bread.
Serves 2-3

Fondue with Bacon

1 clove garlic
2 glasses white wine
1 lb. (4 cups) grated Gruyère cheese
2 teaspoons cornflour (cornstarch)
1 glass Kirsch
1 tablespoon finely chopped parsley
1 teaspoon chopped tarragon
4 tablespoons crisply fried chopped bacon

Rub the sides of the fondue pot with the cut clove of garlic.
Put in the wine and when it is warm add the cheese gradually, stirring in a figure of eight until the mixture bubbles.
Add the cornflour blended smoothly with the kirsch and when the fondue is thick and creamy stir in the herbs and bacon.
Have some French bread cut into pieces and let your guests dip into the fondue as soon as it is ready.
Serves 3-4

Fondue Bengali

1 clove garlic

$\frac{3}{4}$ pint (1$\frac{1}{2}$ cups) dry white
  wine

1 teaspoon lemon juice

1 lb. (4 cups) grated Gruyère
  cheese

$\frac{1}{2}$ lb. (2 cups) grated
  Emmenthal cheese

2 teaspoons cornflour
  (cornstarch)

2 tablespoons curry powder

3 tablespoons Kirsch

white pepper, cayenne pepper

mango chutney

French bread

Rub round the inside of the fondue pot with a cut clove of
garlic. Put in the wine and lemon juice and heat over a low
flame. Add the cheese gradually, stirring all the time and
using a figure of eight motion.

Mix the cornflour and curry powder together and blend
smoothly with the Kirsch.

When the cheese mixture is bubbling, stir in the blended
cornflour and cook until the fondue is thick and creamy.
Add white and cayenne pepper to taste.

Have some pieces of mango from the chutney cut into small
cubes. Spear a cube on to the fondue fork, then a cube of
bread and dip into the fondue.

Serves 4

Meat
Fondues

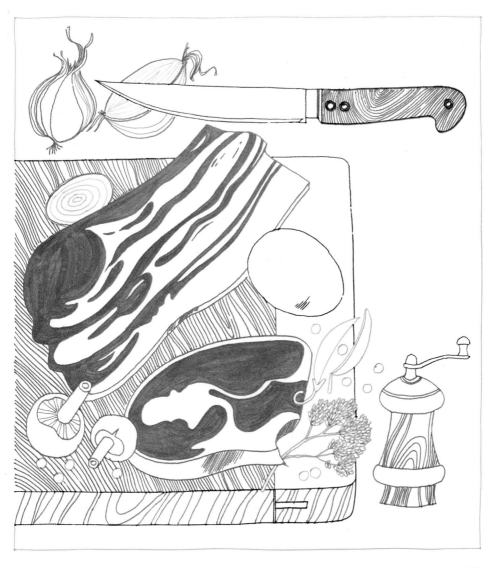

Fondue Bourguignonne

This is not a fondue in the strictest sense of the word and is often given in recipe books as Boeuf Bourguignonne, but the dish originated in the Burgundy district of France and the cooking is done at the table in a fondue pot.

In the foregoing recipes for cheese fondues, an earthenware pot is generally used, but for meat and fish fondues, the pot should be of cast iron, stainless steel or copper.

Oil, preferably vegetable oil, or a mixture of oil and butter is used for the cooking though you will find in the recipe for Oriental Fondue a clear beef stock is needed.

The pan should not be more than $\frac{2}{3}$ filled with oil and a bay leaf or a clove of garlic can be put in if liked, for flavouring. Time can be saved by heating the oil first on the stove and then transferring it to the fondue pot. For successful results the oil should be heated to 375°F. This can be tested by dropping a $\frac{1}{4}$ inch cube of bread into the oil and it should brown in less than one minute.

Only the best quality meat should be used. Cut it into cubes and remove any fat. If there is any doubt about the tenderness of the meat, it can be marinated for several hours in a mixture of oil and red wine – one part oil to two parts red wine and if liked, a little chopped onion. Turn the pieces of meat several times while marinating, then drain and be sure to pat the meat quite dry before cooking, otherwise the moisture will cause the oil to spit.

Be sure to have all the accompaniments ready and provide each guest with a dinner fork as well as his fondue fork so that the cooked meat can be transferred. The fork which has been in the oil would be too hot to use for eating.

The fondue fork should go right through the meat with at least $\frac{1}{4}$ inch showing at the other end. This allows the fork, and not the meat to touch the bottom of the pan so there is no danger of the meat sticking.

Time for cooking depends on the tastes of the guests and you will find they very soon become expert in cooking the meat just as long as they find it suits their taste. While one piece of meat is being eaten another can be put in to cook.

Allow 6-8 oz. fillet steak, beef tenderloin or top sirloin per person. Cut it into 1 inch cubes and remove any fat or sinew.

If a mixture of oil and butter is used, heat the oil first, then add the butter and bring up to the right temperature. Adjust the heat under the pan so that the heat of the fat is maintained throughout the cooking.

A variety of sauces and dips should be provided. Here are some suggestions (you will find the recipes on pages 123-127): Béarnaise sauce, Andalouse sauce, Tartar sauce, Curry sauce, any savoury steak butter and of course, mustard and the usual seasonings.

Have also a tossed green salad, French bread or rolls and if liked, a hot baked potato or potato crisps.

Oriental Fondue

This is similar to the Fondue Bourguignonne but the meat is cooked in clear beef stock.

Use good quality fillet, beef tenderloin or top sirloin steak and cut it into very thin strips. Wrap it round the prongs of the fondue forks and have the beef stock or bouillon boiling in the fondue pan. The steak will cook very quickly and when the meal is finished keep the bouillon. It will be enriched by the steak which has been cooked in it and will make an excellent soup.

Have a selection of the same sauces and accompaniments as suggested for the Fondue Bourguignonne.

Fondue Gitane

In this recipe the meat is cooked in sherry instead of stock or oil.
Use a light cooking sherry and any that remains in the fondue pot can be used up later for soups.
Fillet of veal can be used instead of fillet of beef.

Preparation
Allow 6-8 oz. meat per person and prepare it as for the beef Fondue Bourguignonne.
Have all the accompaniments ready – any mentioned in the previous recipes are suitable. See recipes for Savoury butters, mayonnaise etc. on pages 123-127.

At the table
Have the sherry heating in the fondue pot and allow it to boil before putting in the meat.
Do not add seasoning to the sherry or it will become over seasoned as it continues to boil and reduce.
Spear pieces of meat with the fondue fork and proceed as previously described.

Lamb Fondue

Good quality lamb, cut from the top part of the leg should be used for this fondue. Allow 6-8 oz. meat per person and marinate for as long as possible, preferably over night.

For the marinade

2 tablespoons wine vinegar

4 tablespoons oil

4 tablespoons dry white wine

$\frac{1}{2}$ clove garlic, crushed

1 shallot, peeled and chopped

5-6 peppercorns, crushed

1 sprig rosemary

1 teaspoon finely chopped
mint

Mix all the ingredients for the marinade, add the meat, cut into 1 inch cubes and turn frequently.

When ready to cook, remove the meat and pat as dry as possible. Proceed as for Fondue Bourguignonne and serve with a selection of sauces, e.g. mint sauce, Chinese plum sauce, see page 127 and Chutney butter, see page 126.

Fish
Fondues

Scampi Fondue

Large prawns (shrimp) or scampi are delicious when cooked at the table in a fondue pot.
If frozen fish is used be sure it is well thawed out and dry.
The preparation can be done well in advance and the fish put into the refrigerator until the guests arrive.

$1\frac{1}{2}$-2 lb. prawns or scampi
cornflour (cornstarch)
2 eggs

1 teaspoon soy sauce
breadcrumbs

Preparation
Peel and devein prawns and coat them with cornflour and shake off any excess.
Beat the eggs lightly, stir in the soy sauce. Dip the prawns in the egg then coat with breadcrumbs. Press with the palm of the hand to flatten a little.

At the table
Be sure the oil is hot enough (375°F), then your guests can spear the prawns on their fondue forks and dip them into the hot oil. They will only take a minute or so to heat through.
A Chinese Plum Sauce is very good as a dip; provide some bowls of Remoulade or Tartar sauce as well. See pages 123-127.
Serves 3-4

Chinese Prawns (Shrimp)

This is a variation of the previous recipe.

$1\frac{1}{2}$-2 lb. fresh or frozen
   prawns
2 tablespoons brandy or
   lemon juice
1 teaspoon soy sauce

Batter
2 oz. ($\frac{1}{2}$ cup) all-purpose flour
pinch of salt
1 tablespoon melted butter
1 egg
$\frac{1}{4}$ pint ($\frac{1}{2}$ cup) beer
1 egg white

Preparation
Marinate the prawns in the brandy and soy sauce.
Sift flour and salt into a bowl, stir in the butter and beaten
egg. Add beer gradually and beat until the mixture is smooth.
This can now stand as long as is convenient, then just before
you are ready to go to the table, fold in the stiffly beaten egg
white.

At the table
Let each guest spear a prawn from the marinade with his
fondue fork, dip it in the batter then into the hot oil.
Provide some mayonnaise (see page 124) flavoured with
chopped capers or horseradish or the accompaniments
suggested in the previous recipe.
Serves 3-4

White Fish Fondue

In this recipe the fish is cooked in stock instead of oil.
Fillets of white fish – sole, plaice, cod, fresh haddock etc. are all suitable.

Allow about 6 oz. fish per person

Bouillon

fish trimmings and bones	1 bay leaf
1 onion, peeled and chopped	few sprigs parsley
1-2 sticks celery, chopped	$\frac{1}{2}$ pint (1 cup) dry white wine
1 carrot, peeled and chopped	1-2 teaspoons soy sauce

Preparation

Prepare the fish and cut into $1\frac{1}{2}$-2 inch squares.
Put fish trimmings and bones into a saucepan, add the
vegetables, bay leaf and parsley and just enough water to
cover. Bring to boiling point then skim well. Cover, reduce the
heat and simmer for 30 minutes. Strain and season to taste.

At the table

Pour the fish stock into the fondue pan, add the wine and soy
sauce and heat to boiling point.
Your guests can now spear the pieces of fish and put them into
the boiling stock. They will cook very quickly.
Have some small dishes of soy sauce and chopped cucumber as
accompaniments.

Dessert
Fondues

A dessert fondue is an excellent way of finishing off a meal. It is quick to make and a variety of foods can be used for dipping – fresh or canned fruit, cut into pieces if necessary – sponge or lady fingers or cubes of sponge cake, marshmallows etc.

If you have a choice of pots, use a fairly shallow earthenware one – a metal fondue pot can be used, but care is necessary to see that the creamy mixture does not burn.

Chocolate Nut Fondue

$\frac{1}{2}$ lb. (8 squares) dark
   chocolate
$\frac{1}{4}$ pint ($\frac{1}{2}$ cup) double (heavy)
   cream

4 tablespoons honey
3 oz. ($\frac{3}{4}$ cup) blanched,
   chopped almonds

Preparation
Grate the chocolate and prepare fruit or cake for dipping.

At the table
Put the chocolate, cream and honey into the fondue pot and stir over *very* gentle heat until the chocolate has melted and the mixture is smooth. Stir in the almonds.
Serves 3-4

Chocolate Fondue

$\frac{1}{2}$ lb. (8 squares) Bournville
   (dark) chocolate
2 tablespoons rum or brandy

6 tablespoons double (heavy)
   cream

Break the chocolate into small pieces and put into a pan with the cream. Stir over gentle heat until the chocolate melts and blends with the cream.

Turn off the heat and stir in the rum or brandy.

For variety, chocolate containing fruit and nuts can be used instead of the plain chocolate.

Dubonnet Spice is very good served with this fondue. See recipe on page 122.
Serves 4

38

Chocolate and Orange Fondue

$\frac{1}{2}$ lb. (8 square) Bournville (dark) chocolate
1 small can evaporated milk

2 tablespoons fresh orange juice

Preparation
Turn the chilled evaporated milk into a bowl. Reserve 3 tablespoons and whip the rest until thick. Chill until required.

At the table
Break up the chocolate and put into the fondue pan with the orange juice and the reserved 3 tablespoons milk. Stir over gentle heat until the chocolate has melted and the mixture is smooth.
Remove from the heat and fold in the stiffly whisked cream. Keep warm if necessary over very low heat.
Serves 4

Apricot Cream Fondue

1 large can apricots
1 tablespoon cornflour (cornstarch)
$\frac{1}{2}$ pint (1 cup) double (heavy) cream

$2\frac{1}{2}$ oz. ($\frac{1}{2}$ cup) icing (confectioners) sugar
Sponge fingers, cubes of cake, macaroons etc for dipping

Preparation
Drain the apricots from their syrup and rub through a sieve. Add enough of the syrup to make the quantity up to a scant $\frac{1}{2}$ pint (about $\frac{3}{4}$ cup).

At the table
Mix the cornflour smoothly with a little of the syrup, then put into the fondue pot with all the other ingredients.
Stir over low heat until the mixture is smooth and thick.
Serves 4-5

TABLE
TOP
COOKERY

CHOCOLATE FONDUE (*Photograph: Cadbury Schweppes Food Advisory Service,
Bournville, Birmingham, England*)

TABLE TOP COOKERY

This is another very popular method of entertaining. A variety of light portable table top cookers and dishes are available, which blend utility with gracious design.

Your cooking equipment can be an elaborate electrical fry pan cooker, which can even be used to bake a cake; or a simpler electric fry pan or sauté dish; a chafing dish, either electric or heated with methylated spirit or solid fuel; or just a simple spirit cooker.

A wide variety of casseroles, sauté pans and oven proof glass ware are on the market in every conceivable colour and design. A chafing dish is often fitted with a water bath which could act as a double saucepan and is extremely useful just to keep things hot.

Meals cooked at the table should be simple and well planned. In fact, preparation is the secret of success.

In the recipes which follow you will find some dishes cooked entirely at the table while others need some pre-cooking and the last process or finishing touches done at the table.

Only attempt one hot dish. It is a good plan to have an hors–d'oeuvres or starter course prepared, which your guests can eat while the main dish is cooking and have a cold sweet to follow. Table top desserts are very popular, e.g. crêpes suzettes, but if you choose to cook the sweet at the table, obviously the main course will have been cooked in the kitchen in the ordinary way.

Have as much prepared as you possibly can and have all the accompaniments and ingredients arranged on trays in attractive containers and let your guests help–they will enjoy the party better.

A table heater or plate warmer on the sideboard is very useful for keeping food hot and for any hot accompaniments that may be necessary. If you are using spirit for flaming a dish, for example, it always works better if the spirit is warm, so that could be standing ready on the heater.

Choose the number of guests according to the equipment available. If your fry pan or chafing dish will only take 4-5 pieces of meat it is no good having 6 guests!

Main Dishes

ESCALOPES

Escalopes of veal are small pieces of meat cut from the leg about $\frac{1}{2}$ inch thick. They should be 'batted' or pounded by the butcher until they are very thin and for this reason are ideal for table top cookery – they cook so quickly.
If the butcher has not prepared the escalopes for you, lay each one between two pieces of waxed or oiled greaseproof paper and beat well with a cutlet bat, rolling pin or heavy bottomed fry pan until it is thin. Allow 1 escalope per person unless they are very small. There are a great many ways of serving escalopes, the simplest perhaps is –

Wiener Schnitzel

4 thin escalopes of veal
   (about 5 by 3 inches)
flour
salt, pepper
1 egg
oil
dry white breadcrumbs
butter

Garnish
4 thin slices of lemon
capers, gherkin
lemon juice
chopped parsley

Preparation
Coat the escalopes in seasoned flour and shake off any surplus flour.
Beat the egg, season lightly and add a few drops of oil. Coat the escalopes with the egg and roll in breadcrumbs. Press them on well using a palette knife and set aside until required.

At the table
Heat some oil and butter in the pan, arrange the escalopes without overlapping and cook for 7-10 minutes, turning once.
Put at once on to the serving dish with a slice of lemon, a few capers and a slice of gherkin on the lemon.
Add a squeeze of lemon juice to the butter left in the pan and pour over the escalopes. Sprinkle with chopped parsley.

Wiener Schnitzel with Anchovy Sauce

4 escalopes of veal
juice of 1-2 lemons
flour
salt, pepper
2 egg yolks

fine white breadcrumbs
6 oz. ($\frac{3}{4}$ cup) butter
8 anchovy fillets
1 teaspoon paprika
lemon and olives for garnish

Preparation
Be sure the escalopes are well flattened.
Cover them with lemon juice and leave to marinate for 1 hour.
Drain, coat with seasoned flour and then with egg and bread-crumbs. Refrigerate until required.
Melt half the butter in a small saucepan, add the well mashed anchovies and paprika. Mix well and keep hot.

At the table
Heat the remainder of the butter in the pan, put in the escalopes and brown on both sides, about 7-10 minutes.
Put on to serving plates, pour a little of the anchovy sauce on each one and garnish with a slice of lemon and one or two olives.
Pitted green or stuffed olives are best.
Serves 4

Escalopes à la Crème

1 tablespoon fresh butter
4 escalopes of veal
$\frac{1}{2}$ small onion, finely chopped
4 oz. (2 cups) sliced button
  mushrooms
1 glass white wine
3 tablespoons white stock

salt, pepper
beurre manié (2 tablespoons
  butter kneaded with a
  tablespoon flour)
3 tablespoons double (heavy)
  cream
chopped tarragon

Heat the butter in the pan and when it is foaming, put in the escalopes. Sauté briskly for 3-4 minutes on each side. Remove from the pan. Add the onion and mushrooms, sauté for a few minutes then add the wine. Reduce a little, then replace the meat, add the stock and a little salt and pepper. Bring to the boil, cover and simmer for 5 minutes. Draw away from the heat and add enough beurre manie to thicken, shaking the pan so that it thickens smoothly, reboil and add the cream.
Adjust the seasoning, leave for a minute to reheat and serve. Boil up the sauce and pour over the escalopes. Sprinkle with the tarragon.
Serves 4

Escalopes Palermo

3 tablespoons butter
4 escalopes of veal
1 small onion, peeled and very
  finely chopped
1 glass Marsala wine

1 tablespoon flour
$\frac{1}{4}$ pint ($\frac{1}{2}$ cup) veal stock
$\frac{1}{2}$ teaspoon tomato purée
1 bay leaf
salt, pepper

Heat the butter until it is foaming then put in the escalopes
and sauté for 3 minutes. Add the onion and continue to cook a
further 3 minutes. Add the Marsala, allow it to heat, then
flame.
Remove the escalopes. Stir in the flour, stock and tomato
purée. Bring to boiling point, add the bay leaf and
seasoning.
Replace the veal, cover and simmer for 7-10 minutes.
Serve with creamed spinach.
Serves 4

Escalopes with Orange

2 oz. ($\frac{1}{2}$ stick) butter
4 escalopes of veal
1 tablespoon flour
2 large oranges

1 tablespoon brandy or 1
  small glass sherry
$\frac{1}{4}$ pint ($\frac{1}{2}$ cup) white stock
chopped parsley

Heat the butter, arrange the escalopes in the pan and brown
on both sides. Remove from the pan.
Stir the flour into the butter left in the pan, add the grated
rind and juice of 1 orange, brandy and stock. Bring to boiling
point, season carefully and replace the escalopes. Cover and
simmer for 10 minutes.
Meanwhile, peel the second orange, remove the white pith
and cut into four slices. Serve the escalopes with a slice of
orange on each and pour the sauce over. Sprinkle with parsley.
Serves 4

Piquant Veal Escalopes

4 escalopes of veal
salt, pepper, flour
2 oz. ($\frac{1}{2}$ stick) butter
6 spring (green) onions
   (scallions)

1 lemon, sliced
2 teaspoons rosemary
$\frac{1}{4}$ teaspoon Tabasco
$\frac{1}{4}$ pint ($\frac{1}{2}$ cup) Vermouth
1 tablespoon chopped parsley

Preparation
Pound or bat out the escalopes very thinly and cut each in
half. Coat with seasoned flour and set aside until required.

At the table
Heat the butter until foamy, put in the meat and fry until
golden, turning once. Remove from the pan and keep hot.
Add a little more butter to the pan if necessary and fry the
chopped white part of the onions until soft. Replace the veal,
add the thinly sliced un-peeled lemon, rosemary, Tabasco and
Vermouth. Simmer for 2-3 minutes, then check the seasoning
and sprinkle with the chopped green part of the onions and
chopped parsley.
Serves 4

Escalopes with Fennel

3 tablespoons butter
4 escalopes of veal
salt, pepper
6-8 spring (green) onions
   (scallions), chopped

3-4 tablespoons chopped
   fennel leaves
lemon juice

Heat the butter in the pan until foaming. Put in the meat and
sprinkle with salt, pepper and the chopped onions. Cover and
cook for 7-8 minutes. Sprinkle with the fennel and add a good
squeeze of lemon juice.
Serve the escalopes and spoon the juices left in the pan on top.
A green salad is the best accompaniment.
Serves 4

PIQUANT VEAL ESCALOPES (Photograph: Tabasco Sauce)

Minced Veal Escalopes

Many butchers sell 'pie veal' at a very reasonable price and this can be used to make excellent, inexpensive escalopes.

1 lb. pie veal
2 teaspoons finely chopped
   parsley
1 teaspoon grated lemon rind
salt, pepper
lemon juice
1 egg

flour
2 tablespoons butter
2 tablespoons oil
3 tablespoons dry white wine
   or Vermouth
3 tablespoons white stock

Preparation
Mince or grind the veal and add parsley, lemon rind, salt, pepper and a squeeze of lemon juice. Mix well and bind with the beaten egg. Divide into four portions, flour your hands and shape the meat into balls. Roll in flour and refrigerate for an hour or so.
Flour a rolling pin, and roll out on a floured board to just under $\frac{1}{2}$ inch thick and as nearly as possible into the shape of an escalope. Set aside until required.

At the table
Heat the butter and oil in the pan, put in the escalopes and cook for two minutes on each side. Add the wine, let it bubble for a few seconds then add the stock and simmer for 6-8 minutes.
Put on to serving plates, correct the seasoning of the juices left in the pan, boil up and pour over the escalopes.
Serve with creamed spinach, braised endive or buttered carrots or with a green salad.
Serves 4

Veal Chops Bonne Femme

4 veal chops
3 tablespoons butter
1 gammon rasher, lean
  bacon, or ham strip,
  about $\frac{1}{4}$ lb.
12 button or pickling onions
8 small new potatoes

4 oz. (2 cups) button
  mushrooms, cut into
  quarters
1 tablespoon flour
1 glass white wine
$\frac{3}{4}$ pint ($1\frac{1}{2}$ cups) white stock
salt, pepper, bouquet garni
chopped parsley

Preparation
Trim the chops.
Cut the gammon into strips and blanch with the onions and
potatoes. Drain well.

At the table
Heat the butter in the pan, put in the chops and brown on
both sides then remove from the pan.
Put the gammon strips, onions and mushrooms into the pan
and sauté until the onions begin to colour. Stir in the flour
then add the wine and stock. Bring to boiling point, season
and replace the chops. Add the bouquet garni and potatoes,
cover and simmer for about 15 minutes, or until both meat and
potatoes are tender.
Sprinkle with chopped parsley.
Serves 4

CHICKEN DISHES

Spring chickens and poussins are excellent for cooking at the table. A poussin is a baby chick 4-8 weeks old and spring chickens are generally 8 weeks to 4 months so make very tender eating.

A spring chicken will make two good portions but if the poussins are very small, you may need to allow one per person. In any case, for cooking at table it is best to joint the chickens. They will then cook in 20 minutes or less. A good plan is to serve the first course of the meal while the chicken is cooking. Any of the pieces of equipment mentioned in the introduction to this section can be used – chafing dish, electric fry pan, sauté pan etc.

Chicken Provençal

1 spring chicken or poussin
salt, pepper
flour
corn oil
1 tablespoon finely chopped
  onion

6 tablespoons dry white wine
4 tomatoes, peeled, seeded
  and chopped
1 small clove garlic
1 teaspoon chopped parsley
12 small black olives

Preparation
Joint the chicken and coat with seasoned flour.

At the table
Heat the oil in the chafing pan, put in the chicken and sauté for a few minutes. Add the onion and as soon as it begins to brown add the wine and cook until it is reduced by half. Add the tomatoes, garlic and parsley and continue to simmer for about 15 minutes when the chicken should be tender. Add the olives, allow to heat through and serve with a salad or with mashed potatoes.
Serves 2

Creole Chicken

1 spring chicken
4 tablespoons flour
$\frac{1}{2}$ teaspoon salt
$\frac{1}{8}$ teaspoon white pepper
$\frac{1}{4}$ teaspoon mace
4-5 tablespoons butter
2 tablespoons finely chopped
    onion
$\frac{1}{4}$ pint ($\frac{1}{2}$ cup) chicken stock
$\frac{1}{2}$ teaspoon Worcestershire
    sauce

$\frac{1}{2}$ clove garlic
pinch of thyme
few sprigs parsley
$\frac{1}{2}$ bay leaf
$\frac{1}{4}$ pint ($\frac{1}{2}$ cup) double (heavy)
    cream
2 teaspoons cornflour
    (cornstarch)
1 small can button mushrooms
2-3 tablespoons browned
    slivered almonds

Preparation
Joint the chicken and dry the pieces thoroughly.
Mix the flour, salt, pepper and mace together and coat the
chicken well then shake to remove any surplus flour. Keep in
the refrigerator until required.

At the table
Heat the butter in the dish, put in the chicken joints and
brown all over. Add the onions and cook for 5 minutes. Add
the stock, Worcestershire sauce and flavourings. Bring to
boiling point then cover and cook over low heat for about
15 minutes. Mix the cornflour smoothly with the cream and
stir into the pan. Add the mushrooms, stir until the sauce
thickens, then cook a further 5-10 minutes.
Discard the bay leaf and parsley stalks and stir in the almonds.
This is generally served with rice, so have it ready and
keeping hot.
Serves 2

Chicken with Almonds or Pecans

1 spring chicken, jointed
1 teaspoon salt
$\frac{1}{4}$ teaspoon black pepper
2 tablespoons flour

3 tablespoons butter
3 tablespoons corn oil
$\frac{1}{4}$ teaspoon marjoram
3 oz. (1 cup) almonds

Preparation
Coat the chicken pieces with seasoned flour.

At the table
Heat the butter and oil in the chafing dish. Put in the chicken
and brown on both sides.
Add the marjoram and nuts, cover, and cook over low heat
until the chicken is tender. This will take about 15-20
minutes.
A green salad is a good accompaniment.
Serves 2

Chicken with Herbs

1 spring chicken
2 tablespoons butter
2 teaspoons flour
salt, pepper
6 tablespoons white wine
$\frac{1}{4}$ teaspoon thyme

$\frac{1}{4}$ teaspoon rosemary
1 tablespoon finely chopped
  parsley
1 tablespoon finely chopped
  chives

Preparation
Joint the chicken and dry thoroughly.

At the table
Heat the butter in the pan, put in the chicken joints and
brown all over. Sprinkle with the flour and add a little salt
and pepper. Add the wine and herbs. Turn the chicken over
once or twice and cook over low heat until the chicken is
tender, about 15-20 minutes. Correct the seasoning before
serving.

Country Captain

This recipe comes from an old American cook book. According to this source – Miss Eliza Leslie's 'New Cookery Book' – Country Captain is an East Indian dish, probably first introduced to the British by a captain of the native East Indian troops.

1 spring chicken
4 tablespoons flour
salt, black pepper
3 tablespoons butter
2 tablespoons finely chopped onion
2 tablespoons chopped green pepper

$\frac{1}{2}$ clove garlic, crushed
1 teaspoon curry powder
pinch of thyme
1 small can (1 cup) tomatoes
2 tablespoons seedless raisins
2-3 tablespoons browned almonds

Preparation
Joint the chicken, dry the pieces well and coat with seasoned flour.

At the table
Heat the butter in the pan, put in the chicken pieces and brown on all sides then remove from the pan.
Put the onion, green pepper, garlic, curry powder and thyme into the pan with the butter left from cooking the chicken and stir over low heat for 5 minutes. Add the tomatoes and the juice from the can and return the chicken to the pan. Cover and cook for about 15 minutes or until the chicken is tender. Add the raisins, correct the seasoning and sprinkle the almonds on top.
Chutney is generally served as an accompaniment.
Serves 2

Chicken with White Wine Sauce

1 spring chicken
2 tablespoons flour
salt, black pepper
3 tablespoons corn oil
1 small onion, peeled and
    finely chopped
1 small carrot, peeled and
    grated
1 clove garlic, crushed

1 bay leaf
1 tablespoon chopped parsley
pinch of thyme
$\frac{3}{4}$ pint ($1\frac{1}{2}$ cups) dry white
    wine
$\frac{1}{4}$ lb. (2 cups) sliced
    mushrooms
4 small white onions

Preparation
Joint the chicken, dry thoroughly and coat with seasoned
flour.

At the table
Heat the oil in the pan, put in the chicken pieces and brown
on all sides. Add the onion, carrot and garlic and cook for 10
minutes, stirring frequently. Add the bay leaf, parsley,
thyme and wine. Bring to boiling point, cover and cook for 5
minutes, then add the mushrooms and continue to cook until
the chicken is tender, about 10-15 minutes.
Correct the seasoning and if the sauce is a little thin, stir in
1 teaspoon flour mixed with 1 teaspoon butter.
Serves 2

TOURNEDOS

A tournedos is a small round steak cut from the fillet of beef, and trimmed of all fat. It is an expensive dish, but very good for entertaining on special occasions. The tournedos should be put into a very hot, thick bottomed pan without any fat and browned on both sides. Then a little butter is added and the steaks cooked in all for 4-5 minutes. Béarnaise sauce is the usual accompaniment. See page 125.

Tournedos with Tarragon

4 tournedos
salt, pepper
3 tablespoons butter

2 tablespoons madeira or
  port wine
$\frac{1}{2}$ tablespoon chopped tarragon

Season the tournedos with salt and pepper and brown on both sides in a very hot pan.
Add 2 tablespoons of the butter and cook a further 3 minutes.
Add the madeira, let it bubble for 1 minute then stir in the tarragon and remaining butter.
When it has melted, serve the steaks and pour the liquor over.
Serve with green beans or a salad.
Serves 4

Minute Steak Soubise

Minute steaks are thin slices of entrecôte, especially suitable for table-top cookery as they need to be quickly cooked and only take a few minutes.

4 minute steaks
$\frac{3}{4}$ lb. onions
butter
2 wine glasses red wine
salt, black pepper

$\frac{1}{4}$ pint ($\frac{1}{2}$ cup) single (light) cream
1 teaspoon cornflour (cornstarch)
2 tablespoons stock

Preparation
Flatten the steaks a little if necessary.
Peel the onions and cut into very thin slices. Fry in a little butter until golden brown. Add 1 glass wine and a little salt and pepper and cook for about 5 minutes. Strain off the liquid and reserve it and keep the onions warm.

At the table
Heat a little butter in the pan and when it is foaming put in the steaks and cook them quickly allowing 1-1$\frac{1}{2}$ minutes if required rare and 2-3 minutes if medium rare. Remove from the pan. Add the second glass of wine, bring to boiling point then add the reserved liquid from the onions and cream. Mix the cornflour smoothly with the stock, add to the sauce and stir until boiling. Correct the seasoning then return the steaks and the onions to the pan and just heat through.
Arrange the steaks and some onion on the serving plates and spoon a little of the sauce over the meat.
Serves 4

Steak Diane

1 small onion
2 oz. ($\frac{1}{4}$ cup) butter
4 very thin slices of good
    quality steak, sirloin or
    rump

Worcestershire sauce
brandy
chopped parsley

Peel and chop the onion very finely. Heat the butter in the
chafing dish, add the onion and cook for 1-2 minutes. Put the
steaks into the pan and fry on both sides.
If the steaks are really thin, they will only take a few minutes
to cook.
Add a little Worcestershire sauce and brandy and flame.
Serve the steaks on hot dishes and spoon the liquor left in the
pan on top. Sprinkle with chopped parsley.
Halved tomatoes can be cooked with the steaks if liked.

Sweet and Sour Gammon Rashers

4 gammon rashers or ham
    strips
1 tablespoon butter or lard
4 tablespoons vinegar
2 tablespoons red currant jelly

2 teaspoons made mustard
2 tablespoons light brown
    sugar
2 teaspoons paprika

Preparation
Cut the rind from the bacon and make three or four snips in
the fat so that the rashers will not curl up while cooking.

At the table
Heat the fat in the pan and fry the gammon on both sides until
lightly browned and cooked. Remove from the pan.
Put the rest of the ingredients into the pan and stir well
together. When quite smooth, return the gammon rashers to
the pan and heat through.
Put on to the serving plates and spoon the sauce over.
Serves 4

Steak Au Poivre

2 steaks, entrecôte or rump
   about $\frac{3}{4}$ inch thick
1 tablespoon black
   peppercorns
$\frac{1}{2}$ teaspoon seasoned salt,

1 teaspoon seasoned pepper
corn oil
butter
lemon juice

Preparation

Prepare the steaks at least 2 hours before you are ready to
cook them. Crush the peppercorns with a rolling pin, beat the
steaks lightly, then roll in the peppercorns and press them in
well. Sprinkle with the seasoned salt and pepper, brush with
oil and leave to marinade.

In the picture, you will see the steak is served with fried
tomatoes. If you wish to do this, it would be best to fry the
tomatoes just before your guests arrive, then they can be put
in to the pan with the steaks to reheat at the last minute.

At the table

Heat a little butter in the pan, put in the steaks and cook for
3-4 minutes on each side depending whether your guests like
them rare or medium. Put on to the serving plates, add an
extra tablespoon butter to the pan and swirl it around until it
just begins to colour. Add a squeeze of lemon juice and pour
over the steaks.

Pork Chops with Cider Sauce

4 small pork chops
2 tablespoons light brown
  sugar
1 teaspoon French mustard
2 tablespoons butter
2 teaspoons cornflour
  (cornstarch)

1 large orange
$\frac{1}{2}$ pint (cup) cider
salt, pepper
1 clove garlic, crushed
4 sliced olives
2 cloves
4 rings canned pineapple

Preparation
Trim the chops, removing any excess fat. Snip the edges so
that the chops keep their shape while cooking.
Mix the sugar and mustard together and spread a little on both
sides of the chops. Set aside until required.

At the table
Heat the butter in the pan, put in the chops and brown well
on both sides, then remove.
Stir the cornflour into the fat left in the pan and cook for
1 minute. Add the orange juice and cider, stir until boiling and
boil for 1 minute. Add a little salt and pepper, garlic, olives
and cloves. Return the meat to the pan, cover, and cook for
10-15 minutes or until the meat is tender.
Add the pineapple and just heat through.
Remove the cloves.
Serve the chops with a slice of pineapple on each and spoon
over a little of the sauce.
Serves 4

Sausages in Barbecue Sauce

This is a favourite dish for a teenagers supper party.

1 tablespoon oil or dripping
1 lb. chipolata sausages
$\frac{1}{2}$ small onion, peeled and
   grated finely
2 teaspoons vinegar
1 tablespoon Worcestershire
   sauce

$\frac{1}{2}$ pint (1 cup) tomato juice
2 teaspoons cornflour
   (cornstarch)
few drops Tabasco
little made mustard
salt

Heat the oil in the pan and cook the sausages until brown all over. Add the onion, vinegar, Worcestershire sauce and most of the tomato juice. Use the rest to blend the cornflour smoothly. Heat the contents of the pan for a few minutes then add the blended cornflour and stir until the sauce thickens. Simmer for a few minutes then add the Tabasco, mustard and salt to taste.
Put a cocktail stick into each sausage.
Serves 4

Crumbed Chops

4 New Zealand lamb chops
salt, pepper
rosemary
1 egg
breadcrumbs

2 tablespoons butter
2 tablespoons corn oil
$\frac{1}{2}$ lb. small button mushrooms
2 tomatoes

Preparation
Trim the chops, removing any excess fat. Season with salt and
pepper and tuck one or two leaves of rosemary into the meat
just near the bone. Coat with beaten egg and breadcrumbs and
set aside until required.

At the table
Heat the butter and oil in a pan large enough to take the chops
and mushrooms. When it is foamy, put in the chops and
cook over fairly high heat for two minutes on each side.
Reduce the heat, put the mushrooms into the pan and continue
to cook a further 6-8 minutes.
The tomatoes can be cut in half and put into the pan to heat
during the last 2-3 minutes.
Serves 4

CRUMBED CHOPS (Photograph: New Zealand Lamb Information Bureau)

Sausages with Mexican Dip

This is another teenager favourite, but the sausages should be cooked first and kept warm.
The chafing dish or pan should not be too shallow or the dip will reduce too quickly.

Cooked sausages or
   frankfurters, cut into short
   lengths
3 tablespoons minced
   (ground) onion
3 tablespoons vinegar
$\frac{1}{4}$ pint ($\frac{1}{2}$ cup) tomato ketchup

1 teaspoon Worcestershire
   sauce
juice of $\frac{1}{2}$ lemon
$\frac{1}{2}$ teaspoon paprika
black pepper, salt, sugar

Put the onion and vinegar into the pan and simmer for 5 minutes. Add tomato ketchup, Worcestershire sauce and lemon juice. Simmer a few minutes longer then add paprika, pepper, salt and sugar to taste.
Put cocktail sticks in the sausages and serve with crusty rolls.

Meat Balls in Sour Cream Sauce

1 egg
$\frac{1}{4}$ pint ($\frac{1}{2}$ cup) milk
salt, pepper
2 oz. ($\frac{1}{2}$ cup) dry breadcrumbs
$\frac{1}{2}$ small onion, very finely
    chopped or grated
1 lb. (2 cups) minced (ground)
    lean raw beef

1 tablespoon butter
1 tablespoon flour
1 small can, about 4 oz,
    tomato sauce
$\frac{1}{4}$ pint ($\frac{1}{2}$ cup) sour cream
few small black olives

Preparation
Beat the egg with the milk, seasonings and breadcrumbs, add
about $\frac{1}{4}$ teaspoon of the grated onion and allow to stand for a
few minutes. Add the meat, mix lightly with a fork and shape
into small balls. Cover and store in the refrigerator until
required.

At the table
Heat the butter in the pan and fry the meat balls until brown
all over. Remove from the pan. Add the remaining onion,
sauté for a few minutes then stir in the flour and mix well.
Add the tomato sauce and return the meat balls to the pan.
Simmer for about 10 minutes. Add the sour cream and stir
gently so that the meat balls are well coated with the sauce.
Correct the seasoning, add the olives and leave for a few
minutes to heat through.
Serves 4

Pork with Spicy Orange Sauce

1¼ lb. pork fillet
salt, pepper, flour
2 tablespoons butter
1 small onion, peeled and
   chopped
1 green pepper, blanched,
   seeded and cut into strips

3 oranges
grated rind of ½ orange
1 tablespoon Worcestershire
   sauce
¼ pint (½ cup) stock

Preparation
Trim the meat and cut into 1 inch cubes. Coat with seasoned flour.
Peel one of the oranges, remove all the white pith and cut into segments.

At the table
Heat the butter in the pan, add the onion and green pepper and sauté for 3 minutes. Add the meat and cook for 5 minutes, turning frequently. Add the juice of 2 oranges and ½ teaspoon grated orange rind then add Worcestershire sauce and stock. Bring to boiling point and simmer for 10 minutes, stirring occasionally.
Check the seasoning and add the orange segments just before serving.
A green salad is a good accompaniment.
Serves 4

Burgundy Burgers

1 lb. minced raw beef, chuck
or sirloin (2 cups, ground)
1 teaspoon salt
black pepper
pinch of mixed herbs

1 teaspoon chopped parsley
$\frac{1}{4}$ pint ($\frac{1}{2}$ cup) Burgundy
2 oz. ($\frac{1}{4}$ cup) butter
1 clove garlic

Perparation
Mix the beef, seasoning and herbs with just enough Burgundy
to blend the ingredients together. Cover and set aside for
several hours then just before you are ready to cook, shape
into 6 small cakes and dust lightly with flour.

At the table
Heat the butter and garlic in the chafing dish, put in the
burgers and cook for 3-4 minutes on each side. Remove to hot
plates, discard the garlic and add remaining Burgundy to the
pan. Mix well with the pan juices, and when hot, pour over
the burgers.
French fried potatoes and/or fried onions are a good
accompaniment but these must be prepared beforehand and
kept hot.
Serves 3

Hamburgers

2 small onions
$\frac{1}{2}$ lb. (1 cup) minced (ground)
   beef, chuck or sirloin
seasoned salt,
seasoned pepper
pinch of mixed herbs
1 teaspoon chopped parsley

1 potato, peeled and grated
few drops Worcestershire
   sauce
fat for frying
1 tomato
4 hamburger rolls, English
   muffins or large bread rolls

Preparation
Peel the onions, grate one very finely and cut the other into
very thin rings.
Mix the meat, grated onion, seasonings, herbs, grated potato
and Worcestershire sauce and bind all the ingredients well
together. Divide the mixture into four parts and shape each
into a round flat cake.

At the table
Heat some fat in a pan large enough to take the four
hamburgers and the sliced onion.
Cook the hamburgers for about 4 minutes on one side then
turn over and add the sliced onion. Cook a further 5-6 minutes
when the meat should be cooked and the onion rings soft and
golden brown.
Have the rolls ready on the serving plates, put a hamburger
on each and top with a few onion rings. Garnish with a slice of
tomato.
Makes 4

Beef Stroganoff

This is an excellent dish for entertaining but it needs fairly long cooking, so have it prepared and simmering on the table when your guests arrive. The stroganoff is generally served with noodles or rice so have this prepared and kept hot or serve with a salad.

1 lb. good quality stewing beef
2 oz. (1 stick) butter
2 small onions, peeled and finely chopped
$\frac{1}{4}$ lb. sliced mushrooms

salt, black pepper, nutmeg
$\frac{1}{2}$ teaspoon basil
$\frac{1}{4}$ pint ($\frac{1}{2}$ cup) beef stock
$\frac{1}{2}$ pint (1 cup) sour cream
2 tablespoons finely chopped parsley or chives

Cut the meat into thin slices and then into strips. Heat the butter in the pan, add the onions and sauté until transparent. Add the meat and brown over fairly high heat. Reduce the heat and add the mushrooms, salt, pepper, pinch of nutmeg, basil and stock. Bring to the boil, then cover and simmer for about 45 minutes. Add the cream, check the seasoning and reheat but do not allow the mixture to boil at this stage. Sprinkle with parsley or chives.
Serves 4

Quick Beef Stroganoff

1 tablespoon butter
1 tablespoon corn oil
$1\frac{1}{2}$ lb. (3 cups) minced
  (ground) beef
$\frac{1}{2}$ pint (1 cup) water

1 package Lawry's Beef
  Stroganoff Mix
$\frac{1}{4}$ pint ($\frac{1}{2}$ cup) sour cream
2 tablespoons tomato purée

Heat the butter and oil until foamy. Add the meat and stir
until it browns.
Pour off any excess fat, then add the water and Stroganoff
Mix. Stir well and bring to the boil. Cover, and simmer for
about 25 minutes. Add the cream and tomato purée and
re-heat without boiling.
Serves 5-6

Spicy Mince

1 lb. (2 cups) minced
  (ground) beef
2 tablespoons butter
1 small can condensed
  tomato soup
1 onion, peeled and very
  finely chopped

2 tablespoons water
$\frac{1}{2}$ teaspoon chilli powder
salt, black pepper
pinch of cayenne pepper
1 clove garlic, crushed
1 small can baked beans

Preparation
Brown the meat in the butter. (This is not essential, but it will
save a little time. If the meat is not browned beforehand
allow an extra 5 minutes cooking time).

At the table
Rub over the bottom of the pan with a little butter. Put in all
the ingredients and cook over low heat for about 10 minutes.
Stir occasionally while cooking.
Serve with hot garlic or herb bread. See pages 125-126.
Serves 4

Chilli Con Carne

This really needs to cook for ¾-1 hour at least, so prepare it beforehand and have it simmering over low heat when your guests sit down to their first course.

It should be hot and spicy, but use chilli powder with discretion. Different brands vary in strength but a little extra can be added half way through the cooking if necessary. Lawry's Chilli Seasoning Mix is a good and convenient addition to Chilli Con Carne. If you prefer to use this, omit the garlic, chilli powder and basil as given in the following recipe.

2 tablespoons corn oil
1 onion, peeled and chopped
1 clove garlic, crushed
1 lb. (2 cups) minced
  (ground) raw beef
1 small green pepper, seeded
  and chopped
1 can tomatoes (14-16 oz.)

1 pint (2 cups) water
1 bayleaf
½ teaspoon chilli powder
pinch of basil
salt, pepper
1 can (10-12 oz.) red kidney
  beans

Heat the oil in a fairly large pan, add the onion and garlic and sauté for a few minutes. Add the meat and green pepper and cook until the meat begins to brown. Add all the other ingredients except the kidney beans, bring to boiling point, then reduce the heat and simmer gently – uncovered – until the sauce has thickened, about ½ hour. Add the beans, correct the seasoning, cover, and continue to cook for a further 15-30 minutes.

Serves 4

CHILLI CON CARNE (*Photograph: Lawry's Foods Inc.*)

Devilled Kidneys

6 oz. (1 cup) rice
8 lamb's kidneys
salt, pepper, flour
2 teaspoons made mustard
1 teaspoon Worcestershire
 sauce
2 oz. ($\frac{1}{2}$ stick) butter

4 oz. (2 cups) mushrooms,
 sliced
1 tablespoon brandy
$\frac{1}{4}$ pint ($\frac{1}{2}$ cup) canned
 consommé
pinch of dried tarragon
3 tablespoons double (heavy)
 cream

Preparation
Cook the rice in the ordinary way and keep hot. Soak kidneys
in iced water for 20 minutes, then dry well, skin, cut in half
and remove the hard core. Set aside until ready to use.

At the table
Spread the kidneys with a little mustard, sprinkle the
Worcestershire sauce, and coat them lightly with seasoned
flour.
Heat the butter in the pan, put in the kidneys and cook for
4 minutes. Pour over the brandy, leave it to heat for a moment
then ignite. Shake the pan carefully until the flames have died
down, then add the mushrooms and cook over low heat for
2 minutes. Add the consommé and tarragon, cook a few
minutes longer then stir in the cream. Heat through but do not
let the mixture boil.
Serve on the hot rice.
Serves 4

Nasi Goreng

There are many variations of this Indonesian dish which should be hot and spicy. The one in the picture had strips of pancake across the top but this can be omitted.

$\frac{1}{2}$ lb. onions, peeled and finely chopped
4 oz. ($\frac{1}{2}$ cup) butter
$\frac{1}{2}$ lb. (1 cup) cooked pork or ham diced
2-3 tablespoons curry powder
pinch of cayenne pepper
small pinch of chili powder

2 tablespoons Worcestershire or soy sauce
few drops Tabasco
salt
$\frac{3}{4}$ lb. (2$\frac{1}{2}$ cups) cooked rice
$\frac{3}{4}$ lb. (2 cups) mixed cooked vegetables
2-3 tomatoes

Preparation
Cook the onions in half the butter until translucent and quite soft.

At the table
Heat half the remaining butter in the pan, add the onions and meat and heat together for a few minutes. Add the curry powder and all the seasonings and stir over low heat for 5 minutes. Add the remaining butter, rice and vegetables. Stir all well together until the mixture is hot and well blended. Arrange thin wedges of tomato and strips of pancake, if used, on the top and heat for a further few minutes before serving.
Serves 5-6

Cheese and Tomato Medley

2 onions, peeled and chopped
1 clove garlic, crushed
2 oz. ($\frac{1}{4}$ cup) butter
$\frac{1}{2}$ lb. bacon, chopped
$\frac{1}{4}$ lb. sliced mushrooms
1 14 oz. can ($1\frac{2}{3}$ cups)
   tomatoes

1 large can ($2\frac{1}{2}$ cups) potatoes,
   drained and sliced
salt, pepper
6 oz. ($1\frac{1}{2}$ cups) Gouda or
   Edam cheese, grated

Preparation
Cook the onion and garlic in half the butter until quite soft.

At the table
Heat the remaining butter in the dish (you will need a good sized one), add the cooked onion, bacon and mushrooms and stir over the heat for 5-10 minutes. Add the contents of the can of tomatoes, potatoes and seasoning. Stir well and cook a further 3 minutes.
Stir in most of the cheese and as soon as it melts the medley is ready to serve. Sprinkle the rest of the cheese on top.
Serves 4

Calf's Liver in White Wine

$\frac{3}{4}$ lb. calf's liver
$1\frac{1}{2}$ tablespoons flour
salt, pepper
$\frac{1}{2}$ small onion

$\frac{1}{2}$ small green pepper
1 tablespoon chopped parsley
4 tablespoons butter
3 tablespoons white wine

Preparation
Cut the liver into very thin slices and coat with seasoned flour.
Mince the onion and green pepper.

At the table
Heat half the butter in the chafing dish, put in the slices of
liver and brown on both sides over fairly high heat.
Remove to a hot dish. Put the onion and green pepper into
the chafing dish and sauté over more gentle heat until just
tender. Add the wine, simmer for a few minutes then add the
remaining butter. Return the slices of liver to the pan and heat
through. Sprinkle with parsley.
Serves 3

Spanish Rice

1 tablespoon corn oil
1 tablespoon butter
1 small onion
$\frac{1}{2}$ lb. ($1\frac{2}{3}$ cups) long grain rice
1 pint (2 cups) chicken stock
pinch of saffron

1 small green pepper, blanched, seeded and chopped
1 canned pimento, chopped
2 tomatoes, peeled, seeded and chopped
1 can shrimps or prawns
seasoning

Preparation
Heat the oil and butter in a saucepan, add the onion and sauté until transparent. Add the rice, stir over low heat for a few minutes, then add the stock and saffron. Bring to boiling point, then cover and cook until all the liquid has been absorbed. (about 20 minutes)

At the table
Brush the pan with a little oil or melted butter. Put in the rice and add the green pepper, pimento, tomatoes and shrimps. Mix well and stir occasionally over gentle heat until the mixture is well heated through.
A little extra stock may be needed if the rice is not sufficiently moist.
Serves 3-4

SPANISH RICE (Photograph · Cookpot ov Aubeca)

Paupiettes of Liver

$\frac{1}{2}$ lb. calf's liver

$\frac{1}{2}$ lb. rashers of bacon

black pepper

lemon juice

thyme

2 tablespoons butter

1 teaspoon flour

6 tablespoons Marsala

4 tomatoes, peeled and
   chopped

4 tablespoons stock

Preparation

Cut the liver into very thin slices a little smaller than the bacon rashers. Season with black pepper and a squeeze of lemon juice and put 3-4 leaves of thyme on top. Roll up with the bacon on the outside and secure with cocktail sticks.

At the table

Heat the butter in the chafing dish, add the paupiettes and sauté for a few minutes. Stir in the flour, add the Marsala and let it bubble for a minute or so then add the tomatoes and stock. Cover and cook gently for about 5-7 minutes.

These can be served with potato crisps and a green salad.

Serves 4

Liver and Bacon Rolls

This is a simpler version of the preceding recipe for Paupiettes of Liver.

$\frac{1}{2}$ lb. calf's liver

$\frac{1}{4}$ lb. rashers of streaky bacon

fresh sage leaves

butter

Cut the liver into thumb sized pieces. Flatten out the rashers of bacon and cut into halves.

Roll half a rasher of bacon round the liver with a sage leaf in between.

Secure with a cocktail stick or thread on to skewers. Heat some butter in the chafing dish, put in the liver balls and cook until well browned. If you are using skewers, turn them frequently.

Serve with Sage Butter.

Work 3 teaspoons chopped fresh sage into 4 oz. ($\frac{1}{2}$ cup) butter, add 1 teaspoon lemon juice and a little freshly milled pepper.

Serves 3-4

Fried Rice

This is often served as an accompaniment to Chinese dishes, but it makes an excellent supper dish to cook at the table.

$\frac{1}{2}$ lb. ($1\frac{1}{3}$ cups) long grain rice
1 tablespoon corn oil
$\frac{1}{2}$ lb. (1 cup) cooked pork, diced
few prawns (shrimp)
1 egg
1 teaspoon soy sauce
1 teaspoon water
2-3 spring (green) onions
$\frac{1}{4}$ lb. ($\frac{1}{2}$ cup) cooked ham, chopped

Preparation
Boil the rice, allowing plenty of time for it to dry out.

At the table
Heat the oil, add the pork and fry for 2 minutes, then add the rice and stir continuously until it is quite hot, about 8-10 minutes. Add prawns and lightly beaten egg and stir carefully through the rice. Add the soy sauce mixed with the water and the chopped spring onions.
Sprinkle with the ham and allow another minute or so for all to heat through before serving.
Serves 3-4

Chafing Dish Lobster

3 tablespoons corn oil
6-8 (green) spring onions (scallions)
2 tomatoes, peeled and quartered
salt, pepper
1 small glass dry white wine or vermouth
meat from 1 cooked lobster, cut into squares
lemon juice

Heat the oil in the chafing dish, add the bulbous part of the onions whole, leave for 1 minute then add the tomatoes and seasoning and cook for 2 minutes. Add the wine and when it bubbles add the lobster. Let it heat through gently, then sprinkle with lemon juice and the chopped green part of the onions.
Serves 2

Lobster Newburg

As only the tail meat is used for this dish, the rest of the lobster meat can be used for another dish e.g. lobster mayonnaise.

1 cooked lobster
salt, pepper
$\frac{1}{4}$ pint ($\frac{1}{2}$ cup) Madeira
2 oz. ($\frac{1}{4}$ cup) butter

$\frac{1}{4}$ pint ($\frac{1}{2}$ cup) double (heavy) cream
3 egg yolks

Remove the meat from the tail of the lobster, discard the membrane and cut into even slanting slices.
Arrange in a well buttered chafing dish, season with salt and pepper and heat through, turning once.
Add the wine and keep over medium heat until it has reduced by about two thirds.
Beat the egg yolks and cream together and pour over the lobster. Leave for a minute or so to heat through then turn off the heat and add the butter a little at a time.
Serve with a green salad.
Serves 2

Prawns (Shrimp) with Spinach

1 lb. spinach
4 oz. (1 cup) prawns
2 tablespoons butter

2 hard boiled eggs
4-5 tablespoons cream
salt, pepper, grated nutmeg

Preparation
Cook the spinach, drain very thoroughly and chop fairly coarsely.

At the table
Melt the butter in the chafing dish, add the spinach, season with salt, pepper and grated nutmeg and heat through.
Put the prawns and sliced hard boiled eggs on top, and pour the cream over. Cover the pan and cook for 3-4 minutes.
Serves 2

Omelettes

Note *When making an omelette avoid using too large a pan. For 3-4 eggs the pan should be not more than 7 inches in diameter.*

Country Ham Omelette

4 eggs
1 tablespoon cold water
salt, pepper
1 teaspoon chopped parsley

$\frac{1}{2}$ teaspoon chopped tarragon
1 tablespoon butter
4 oz. ($\frac{1}{2}$ cup) chopped cooked
   ham

Break up the eggs lightly with a fork, add water, seasoning and herbs.
Heat the butter in the pan, pour in the egg mixture, stir two or three times and lift the edges so that the uncooked mixture runs on to the bottom of the pan. While the top is still moist, sprinkle with the chopped ham. Fold the omelette over and sprinkle a little more parsley on top.
Serves 2

Cheese and Bacon Omelette

4 eggs
salt, pepper
1 tablespoon double (heavy)
   cream
4 tablespoons grated Gruyère
   cheese

2 rashers crisply cooked
   bacon
1 tablespoon butter

Break the eggs up lightly with a fork, add salt, pepper and cream. Add the cheese and crumbled bacon and mix well. Melt the butter in the pan and when foaming pour in the egg mixture. Cook as described in the previous recipe for Country Ham Omelette.
Serves 2

Herb Frittata

$\frac{1}{4}$ of a Spanish onion, peeled
  and finely chopped
corn oil
3-4 eggs
2 teaspoons finely chopped
  parsley

2 teaspoons finely chopped
  mint
2 teaspoons finely chopped
  basil
salt, black pepper
butter

Preparation
Sauté the onion in a little oil until quite soft and transparent.

At the table
Beat the eggs lightly, add the cooked onion, herbs and
seasoning. Heat a little butter and oil in the pan, pour in the
egg mixture and cook until lightly browned on the under side.
Add a little more butter if necessary, turn, and cook the other
side.
Serves 2

Kidney Omelette

1 calf's kidney	$\frac{1}{4}$ pint ($\frac{1}{2}$ cup) stock
3 tablespoons butter	3 tablespoons Madeira
1 tablespoon cornflour (cornstarch)	3 eggs
	salt
1 tablespoon peeled chopped shallot	few drops Tabasco
	1 tablespoon chopped parsley

Preparation
Skin the kidney, remove any fat and hard core, split in half and cut into thin slices.
Heat 2 tablespoons of the butter in a small pan until it just begins to colour. Put in the kidney and cook for 4 minutes. Heat the remaining butter in a saucepan, stir in the cornflour, mix well, add the shallot and cook for 1 minute. Add the stock and wine, stir until boiling and boil for 1 minute. Add the kidney, correct the seasoning and either keep hot or re-heat when you are ready to make the omelette.

At the table
Beat the eggs lightly, add a pinch of salt, Tabasco and parsley. Heat 1 tablespoon butter in the omelette pan, pour in the egg mixture and using a fork stir with a circular motion about 7 times until the omelette is set underneath and slightly runny on top. Fold the omelette over, spoon the hot kidney sauce round and sprinkle with parsley.
Serves 2

KIDNEY OMELETTE (Photograph · Tabasco Sauce)

Pipérade

1 green pepper, seeded and
   sliced
corn oil
4 tomatoes, peeled, seeded
   and chopped
1 small onion, peeled and
   sliced

$\frac{1}{2}$ clove garlic, crushed
3 tablespoons chopped cooked
   ham
seasoning
1 tablespoon butter
4 eggs

Preparation
Sauté the green pepper for a few minutes in a little oil. Add
the tomatoes, onion, garlic and ham. Season lightly with salt
and pepper. Add the butter and cook all slowly until the
vegetables are quite soft.

At the table
Brush the pan with a little oil, put in the vegetable and ham
mixture and heat thoroughly.
Beat the eggs lightly with a little salt and pepper and pour into
the pan. Stir occasionally until the mixture has the consistency
of soft scrambled egg.
Serves 2

Omelette Grand'Mere

This is a classic omelette and while it appears to be so simple is delicious to eat. The crisp cubes of bread in the centre are a contrast to the smooth creaminess of the eggs.

2 slices of white bread
butter
4 eggs

salt, pepper
1 tablespoon cold water
2 tablespoons grated cheese

Preparation
Remove the crusts from the bread and cut it into small cubes. Fry until crisp in a little butter and keep hot.

At the table
Beat the eggs lightly with a fork, add salt, pepper and water. Heat a little butter in the pan, pour in the eggs, lifting the edges with the fork as it begins to set. When the middle is barely set, put the cubes of bread in the centre, sprinkle with the cheese and fold over.

Serves 2

Spanish Omelette

1 small onion, chopped
1 clove garlic, crushed
2 tablespoons corn oil
3 small potatoes, boiled and
   chopped
2-3 tablespoons cooked peas
1 canned pimento, chopped

1 tomato, peeled, seeded and
   chopped
3 eggs
$\frac{1}{2}$ teaspoon Tabasco
salt, pepper
pinch of mixed herbs

Preparation
Sauté the onion and garlic in 1 tablespoon oil until soft. Set aside until required.

At the table
Mix all the vegetables, including the onion and garlic, together in a bowl.
Pour 1 tablespoon oil into the omelette pan, add the vegetables and heat thoroughly.
Beat the eggs lightly, add Tabasco and seasoning and pour into the pan over the vegetables. Stir lightly, then leave until the eggs are just set.
Sprinkle with herbs and the omelette is ready to serve.
Serves 2

SPANISH OMELETTE (Photograph: Tabasco Sauce)

Spaghetti and Cheese Omelette

3 eggs, separated
salt, pepper
1 can (8 oz.) spaghetti with
    tomato and cheese sauce

2 tablespoons butter
2 oz. ($\frac{1}{2}$ cup) grated Cheddar
    cheese

Preparation

This omelette only takes a few minutes to make and can quite
well be done at the table – but if you prefer you could have
the eggs separated and beat the whites stiffly beforehand.
If you cover the bowl with a plate and turn it upside down,
the egg white will keep stiff for an hour or more.

At the table

Mix the egg yolks with a little salt and pepper and add the
spaghetti with tomato and cheese sauce. Fold in the stiffly
beaten egg whites.
Heat the butter in the pan, pour in the egg mixture and cook
for 3-4 minutes until the underside is lightly browned.
Sprinkle the grated cheese on top and cook a further 2-3
minutes until the cheese melts.
This omelette is not folded over.
Serve with a salad.
Serves 2

Jam Omelette

2 tablespoons apricot jam
3 tablespoons rum
4 large eggs
1 tablespoon water
pinch of salt

1 teaspoon sugar
whipped cream to which
    a little sugar and a few
    drops of almond extract
    have been added

Preparation
Measure out the jam and rum and put them in a warm place
while making the omelette.

At the table
Beat up the eggs lightly with a fork, add the water, salt and
sugar.
Heat the butter in the omelette pan and when frothy, pour in
the eggs. Lift the edges of the omelette with the fork as it
begins to set so that the runny part on top will trickle down
into the pan. When the middle is barely set, put in the warm
jam and fold the omelette in half. Pour over the warm rum and
flame.
Serve with the sweetened and flavoured cream.
Serves 2

Omelette Paysanne

1 tablespoon butter
4 tablespoons diced salt pork
4 tablespoons diced cooked
  potatoes
1 teaspoon finely chopped
  parsley

1 teaspoon finely chopped
  chives
salt, pepper
4 eggs

Heat the butter in the pan, put in the pork and fry until lightly browned. Remove to a plate. Put the potatoes into the pan and fry till golden. Return the meat to the pan and add the parsley and chives and a little seasoning.

Pour the beaten eggs over the mixture, stir two or three times with a fork and cook until the centre of the omelette is just set but still moist. Fold over carefully.

Serves 2

Omelette Aux Cerises

$\frac{1}{2}$ lb. ripe cherries
2 tablespoons kirsch
4 eggs
1 tablespoon cold water

1 tablespoon butter
1 tablespoon sugar
icing (confectioners) sugar

Preparation
Stone the cherries and marinate them in the kirsch for 1-2 hours.

At the table
Beat the eggs lightly with the water, add the cherries and the liqueur in which they have been marinating and the sugar. Heat the butter in the pan and make the omelette in the usual way. Fold over and sprinkle with the icing sugar.

Serves 2

Pancakes and Waffles

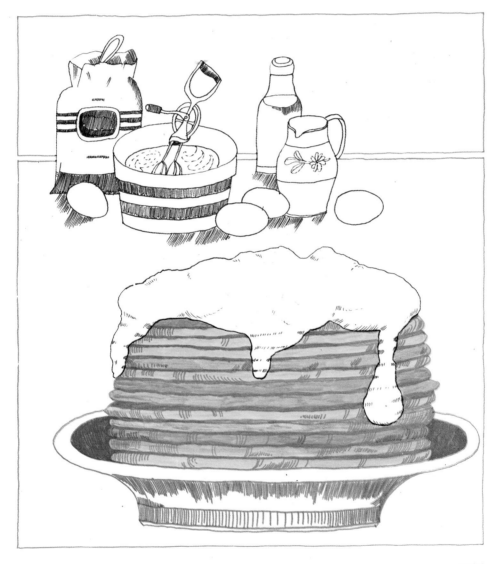

Apple Pancakes with Loganberry Sauce

These are fun to make, but you will need facilities to keep them hot.

5 oz. ($1\frac{1}{4}$ cups) flour
1 teaspoon baking powder
$\frac{1}{2}$ teaspoon salt
2 oz. ($\frac{1}{4}$ cup) sugar
1 egg
about 8 fluid oz. (1 cup) milk
2 oz. ($\frac{1}{4}$ cup) butter, melted
2-3 dessert apples, peeled,
  cored and finely chopped

$\frac{1}{4}$ teaspoon cinnamon
Loganberry Sauce
1 can loganberries
4 oz. ($\frac{1}{2}$ cup) sugar
4 cooking apples, peeled,
  cored and chopped

To make the batter
Sift the flour, baking powder, salt and sugar together.
Beat the egg, add milk and melted butter and use to make a
smooth batter. Beat well, stir in the apples and cinnamon.

To make the sauce
Drain the loganberries and put $\frac{1}{4}$ pint ($\frac{1}{2}$ cup) of the juice in
a pan with the sugar. Heat until the sugar has dissolved. Add
the apples and cook until soft. Add the loganberries, simmer
for 5 minutes, then put all through a sieve.

Preparation
Make the batter mixture and the sauce.

At the table
Heat a little butter in a thick bottomed pan. Drop in a large
tablespoon of the batter and cook until bubbles appear on top
and the underside is brown.
Turn over and brown the other side.
Keep hot while cooking the rest of the batter.
Serve with the hot loganberry sauce.
Serves 4

102

Apricot Pancakes

Pancakes made with $\frac{1}{2}$ pint
  (1 cup) batter: see page 123
1 lb. fresh apricots
$\frac{1}{2}$ pint (1 cup) water
6 tablespoons sugar

3 tablespoons blanched and
  shredded almonds
3-4 tablespoons double
  (heavy) cream

Preparation
Make the pancakes.
Cut the apricots in halves, stone, and cook until tender in the
water and sugar. Remove the fruit and reduce the syrup until
thick.
Toast the almonds.

At the table
Arrange the pancakes on top of one another in the chafing
dish with the apricots in between.
Pour the syrup over and heat through.
Cut into four sections to facilitate serving. Sprinkle with the
almonds and pour the cream on top.
Serves 4

Orange Pancakes

$\frac{1}{2}$ pint (1 cup) pancake batter: see recipe on page 123

$\frac{1}{4}$ lb. (1 stick or $\frac{1}{2}$ cup) unsalted butter

2 oz. ($\frac{1}{4}$ cup) sugar

$\frac{1}{4}$ pint ($\frac{1}{2}$ cup) orange juice

$2\frac{1}{2}$ tablespoons grated orange rind

1 teaspoon lemon juice

3 tablespoons Cointreau

a little orange marmalade

Preparation
Add $\frac{1}{2}$ tablespoon grated orange rind to the batter and make some wafer thin pancakes. Stack them with a piece of grease-proof paper between each until required for use.
Cream the butter and sugar until light and fluffy, beat in the remaining grated orange rind, orange juice, lemon juice and Cointreau.

At the table
Put the sauce into the chafing dish and heat over a low flame. While it is heating, spread each pancake with a little marmalade and roll up. Put the pancakes into the hot sauce and heat through, basting from time to time with the hot sauce.
It will only take a few minutes for the pancakes to heat if they have been made thin enough.

Crêpes Suzettes

Pancakes Follow the usual
  recipe (see page 123) but
  add 1 tablespoon melted
  butter and 1 tablespoon
  brandy to the batter.

Orange Butter
2-3 lumps sugar
1 large orange or 2 tangerines
  when available
3 tablespoons butter
2 tablespoons caster or
  granulated sugar
1 tablespoon orange juice
1 tablespoon orange Curaçao
2-3 tablespoons rum

Preparation
Make the pancakes, wafer thin. Rub the sugar over the orange
to remove the zest, then crush the sugar and put with the
butter, caster sugar, orange juice and Curaçao.

At the table
Put the orange butter into the chafing dish and heat. Fold the
pancakes in four and overlap in the dish. Baste the pancakes
with the sauce whilst heating.
Pour over the rum, leave to heat for a few seconds, then flame.
Serves 4

Party Pancakes

½ pint (1 cup) pancake batter:
    see page 123
2 tablespoons double (heavy)
    cream
1 macaroon, crushed and
    sieved
1 tablespoon rum

Filling
2 bananas
4 slices canned pineapple
4 tablespoons apricot jam
2 tablespoons butter
2 tablespoons icing
    (confectioners) sugar
2 tablespoons rum

Preparation
Make the pancake batter and just before cooking the pancakes
stir the cream, rum and sieved macaroon into the batter.
Make the pancakes as thin as possible.
Slice the bananas, chop the pineapple and bind together with
the jam.

At the table
Heat the butter in the pan. Spread each pancake with some of
the filling, fold in four and arrange, overlapping, in the pan.
Dust with icing sugar and pour over the rum. Leave for a few
seconds to heat then flame.
Serves 4

Crêpes Aux Pommes

2 medium cooking apples
sugar syrup: see page 127
pancakes made with $\frac{1}{2}$ pint
   (1 cup) batter: see page 123
2 oz. ($\frac{1}{4}$ cup) sugar

Sauce
2 oz. ($\frac{1}{4}$ cup) butter
grated rind and juice of
   1 orange
3 tablespoons Cointreau or
   or brandy

Preparation
Peel, core and slice the apples and poach in sugar syrup until
tender.
Make the pancakes and fold round the drained apple slices.

At the table
Melt the butter in the chafing dish, add orange juice, and
sugar and simmer for 4-5 minutes.
Put in the pancakes, pour over the liqueur and heat through.
Sprinkle with orange rind.
Serves 4-5

St. Clements Pancakes

$\frac{1}{2}$ pint (1 cup) pancake batter:
   see page 123
Sauce
2 tablespoons butter
4 oz. ($\frac{1}{2}$ cup) sugar
grated rind of 1 orange

grated rind of 1 lemon
juice of 1 orange
juice of $\frac{1}{2}$ lemon
$\frac{1}{4}$ pint ($\frac{1}{2}$ cup) double (heavy)
   cream
3 tablespoons Cucaçao

Preparation
Make the pancakes and stack until required.

At the table
Put the butter into the chafing dish, add the sugar, grated
orange and lemon rind, orange and lemon juice. Stir over low
heat until the sugar has dissolved.
Stir in the lightly whipped cream and Cucaçao.
Fold the pancakes in four, put into the sauce and reheat,
basting occasionally.
Serve the pancakes with some of the sauce poured over.
Serves 4

WAFFLES

These are fun to make at the table but you will need a special waffle iron. The electrically heated one is more convenient to use because both sides of the waffle are cooked at the same time. If you cook the waffles over your spirit heater, it will be necessary to turn them.

The cooking time varies with different irons but generally, 2-3 minutes is all that is required and your guests can take their turn at cooking their own waffle.

Golden syrup or maple syrup is the most popular accompaniment but fruit syrups and more elaborate fillings can be used. Ice cream may be used as a topping for desserts. Savoury waffles are also popular.

Plain Waffles

4 oz. (1 cup) flour
2 teaspoons baking powder
pinch of salt
2 tablespoons sugar

1 egg – separated
2 teaspoons melted butter
about $\frac{1}{4}$ pint ($\frac{1}{2}$ cup) milk
$\frac{1}{2}$ teaspoon vanilla essence

Preparation
Make the batter as follows but it should not be left to stand too long before use.
Sift all the dry ingredients into a bowl, make a well in the centre and put in the egg yolk and melted butter. Add the milk gradually, beating well to make a smooth batter. Add the vanilla and lastly, fold in the stiffly beaten egg white.

At the table
Heat the iron through evenly, then pour in enough batter to just run over the surface. (A measure is usually supplied with electric waffle irons.) Be careful not to over fill. Close the iron over the mixture and leave for 2-3 minutes. Turn the iron over once if you are not using an electric iron.
When cooked, the waffle should be golden brown and crisp and easily removed from the iron.
Make 3-4 waffles

Sour Milk Waffles

4 oz. (1 cup) flour
1 teaspoon bicarbonate soda
   (baking soda)
2 teaspoons baking powder
salt

1 egg
1 tablespoon melted butter
$\frac{1}{2}$ pint (1 cup) sour milk or
   buttermilk

Preparation
Make the batter.
Sift all the dry ingredients together and make a well in the centre, add the whole egg and the butter and add the milk gradually beating until the mixture is smooth. It should be the consistency of thick cream.

At the table
Proceed exactly as described for plain waffles but serve with butter instead of syrup.
Makes 4 waffles

Pineapple Waffles

4 oz. (1 cup) flour
2 teaspoons baking powder
pinch of salt
2 tablespoons sugar
$\frac{1}{2}$ teaspoon grated lemon rind
4 oz. ($\frac{1}{2}$ cup) drained crushed
    pineapple

1 egg, separated
2 tablespoons melted butter
scant $\frac{1}{4}$ pint (scant $\frac{1}{2}$ cup) milk
$\frac{1}{4}$ pint ($\frac{1}{2}$ cup) syrup from the
    pineapple
extra 2 oz. ($\frac{1}{4}$ cup) sugar

Preparation

Make up the waffle batter but avoid letting it stand too long.
Sift the flour, baking powder, salt and sugar together into a
bowl. Stir in the grated lemon rind and pineapple and mix
well. Make a well in the centre, add the egg yolk and melted
butter and gradually beat in the milk. When the mixture is
quite smooth, fold in the stiffly beaten egg white.
Make the sauce by dissolving the sugar in the pineapple syrup
and boiling it for 5 minutes.

At the table

Cook the waffles as described on page 110.
Serve with the pineapple sauce.
Makes 4 waffles.

WAFFLES

These are fun to make at the table but you will need a special waffle iron. The electrically heated one is more convenient to use because both sides of the waffle are cooked at the same time. If you cook the waffles over your spirit heater, it will be necessary to turn them.

The cooking time varies with different irons but generally, 2-3 minutes is all that is required and your guests can take their turn at cooking their own waffle.

Golden syrup or maple syrup is the most popular accompaniment but fruit syrups and more elaborate fillings can be used. Ice cream may be used as a topping for desserts. Savoury waffles are also popular.

Plain Waffles

4 oz. (1 cup) flour
2 teaspoons baking powder
pinch of salt
2 tablespoons sugar

1 egg – separated
2 teaspoons melted butter
about $\frac{1}{4}$ pint ($\frac{1}{2}$ cup) milk
$\frac{1}{2}$ teaspoon vanilla essence

Preparation
Make the batter as follows but it should not be left to stand too long before use.
Sift all the dry ingredients into a bowl, make a well in the centre and put in the egg yolk and melted butter. Add the milk gradually, beating well to make a smooth batter. Add the vanilla and lastly, fold in the stiffly beaten egg white.

At the table
Heat the iron through evenly, then pour in enough batter to just run over the surface. (A measure is usually supplied with electric waffle irons.) Be careful not to over fill. Close the iron over the mixture and leave for 2-3 minutes. Turn the iron over once if you are not using an electric iron.
When cooked, the waffle should be golden brown and crisp and easily removed from the iron.
Make 3-4 waffles

Desserts

Flaming Cherries with Ice Cream

1 large can red cherries
$\frac{1}{4}$ pint ($\frac{1}{2}$ cup) rum
1 teaspoon Curaçao

1 teaspoon cornflour
(cornstarch)

Preparation
Drain and pit the cherries and marinate them in the rum for several hours.
Boil the cherry juice until it has reduced to about $\frac{2}{3}$ the original quantity.

At the table
Heat the cherry juice, add the cornflour, mixed to a smooth paste with a little cold water, stir until boiling and boil for 1 minute. Add the cherries, rum and Curaçao.
Check to make sure no sugar is required (it depends on the heaviness of the cherry juice).
When the mixture is very hot, flame, and as the flames begin to die down serve over portions of ice cream.
Serves 5-6

Mocha Sauce

This is a rich dessert sauce to make at the table and serve hot with ice cream or with a salad of pineapple. pears and bananas.

1 can evaporated milk
2 teaspoons instant coffee
2 oz. ($\frac{1}{4}$ cup) sugar

4 oz. (4 squares) plain
chocolate
2 teaspoons rum

Put the milk, coffee, sugar and grated chocolate into the fondue pan. Stir until the mixture boils then reduce the heat and simmer gently for 5 minutes, stirring constantly.
Stir in the rum.
Serves 4

Bananas Burgundian

4-5 bananas
juice of 1 lemon
$\frac{1}{2}$ pint (1 cup) Burgundy
4 oz. (1 cup, lightly packed)
   brown sugar
1 teaspoon grated orange rind

$\frac{1}{2}$ teaspoon ground nutmeg
$\frac{1}{2}$ teaspoon ground cinnamon
3 tablespoons flaked almonds
4 tablespoons rum

Preparation
Just before your guests sit down to their meal, peel the
bananas, brush them all over with lemon juice and leave
covered, standing in any lemon juice that may be left.

At the table
Put the Burgundy, sugar, orange rind and spices into the
chafing pan and stir over gentle heat until the sugar has
melted. Put in the bananas and cook until they are just tender.
Sprinkle with the almonds, pour over the rum, let it heat for
a moment or so then ignite.
Serve with cream or ice cream.
Serves 4-5

Flamed Peaches

2 tablespoons sugar
2 oz. ($\frac{1}{2}$ stick) butter
1 large orange
8 canned peach halves

little peach juice
1 tablespoon sherry
3 tablespoons brandy

Have a chafing dish or pan large enough to hold the fruit
without overlapping.
Put in the sugar and heat until it just begins to take colour.
Add the butter and orange juice and arrange the peaches in
the pan. Add 1-2 tablespoons peach syrup, and pour over the
brandy. Leave a few seconds to heat, then flame.
A maraschino cherry put into the centre of each peach gives
added attraction.

Glazed Apples

$\frac{1}{2}$ pint (1 cup) water
juice of 1 lemon
strip of lemon peel
4 oz. ($\frac{1}{2}$ cup) sugar

4 medium sized cooking
   apples
1 tablespoon Curaçao
2 tablespoons butter

Preparation
Put the water, lemon juice, lemon peel and sugar into a pan
and bring to boiling point.
Peel the apples and poach very carefully in the syrup until
tender.

At the table
Pour the syrup into the chafing dish, add Curaçao and butter.
Put in the apples and baste with the syrup until warmed
through.
Serves 4

Peach Dessert

2 oz. ($\frac{1}{2}$ stick) unsalted butter
8 canned peach halves
6 tablespoons brandy

$\frac{1}{4}$ pint ($\frac{1}{2}$ cup) syrup from
   the peaches
$\frac{1}{2}$ pint (1 cup) double (heavy)
   cream

Heat the butter in the pan and when it is foaming put in the
peaches and allow them to brown on both sides. Add half the
brandy, leave it to heat for a moment then ignite. Extinguish
the flame before it dies out and arrange the peaches on warm
plates.
Add the peach syrup to the butter left in the pan, add the
remaining brandy and bring to boiling point, Add the cream,
reduce the heat a little and stir until the sauce thickens. Pour it
over the peaches.
Serves 4

Apricots Jubilee

This is a delicious addition to ice cream. Ice cream of any flavour can be used, but it is particularly good with banana or lemon flavoured ice cream.

1 large can apricot halves
2 slices lemon
$\frac{1}{4}$ teaspoon powdered cloves

4-5 tablespoons brandy
ice cream
4-5 macaroons

Preparation
Drain off the apricot juice. Put it into a pan with the lemon and cloves and boil until the quantity is reduced by half. Crush the macaroons.

At the table
Strain the apricot juice into the pan, add the apricots and brandy and keep over medium heat until hot. Flame and pour over the ice cream. Sprinkle each portion with the macaroon crumbs.
Serves 5-6

Flaming Apples

4 dessert apples, peeled,
    cored and thinly sliced
2 oz. ($\frac{1}{4}$ cup) butter

brown sugar
3 tablespoons rum
2 tablespoons apple jelly

Melt the butter in the chafing dish, put in the apples and cook until well browned on both sides. This should only take a few minutes.
Sprinkle with sugar and add the rum. Heat for a few seconds then flame. When the flames have died down remove the apples to serving plates. Stir the apple jelly into the mixture left in the pan and when melted, pour over the apples.
Serve with whipped cream.
Serves 4

118

Glazed Pineapple

4 slices fresh pineapple,
  about $\frac{1}{2}$ inch thick
3 oz. ($\frac{3}{8}$ cup) unsalted butter
4 tablespoons Kirsch

4 oz. (1 cup, lightly packed)
  brown sugar
2 tablespoons rum

Preparation
Remove the peel and hard core from the pineapple, pour over
the Kirsch and leave to marinate for an hour or so.

At the table
Heat the butter in the pan, put in the pineapple and Kirsch
and keep over low heat for 7-10 minutes.
Sprinkle with the sugar, add the rum and ignite. When the
flame has died down, put the pineapple on to plates and spoon
over the liquid left in the pan.
Serve with whipped cream.
Serves 4

Note Canned pineapple can be used if preferred. Allow 2 slices per
person and reduce the sugar to half quantity. The canned pineapple
will only need a few minutes to heat through.

Café Brulot

This makes a delightful end to a meal which has been cooked in the ordinary way. Your guests will be relaxed and will enjoy sitting round the table while it is being prepared. For the best dramatic effect, prepare the Café Brulot by dim candlelight.

1 orange
1 tablespoon sugar
1 stick cinnamon (2-3 inch length)

few cloves
$\frac{1}{8}$ pint ($\frac{1}{4}$ cup) brandy
1 pint strong black coffee

Preparation
Cut the orange into quarters, remove the peel and blanch it. Remove all white pith and cut the peel into thin shreds.

At the table
Put the orange shreds, sugar, spices and brandy into the chafing dish and leave over medium heat until the brandy is hot then flame. Allow to blaze for a few minutes, then stir very carefully to blend the flavours. When the flames die out add the coffee and when hot serve in small cups.
Serves 3-4

Drinks

Dubonnet Spice

$\frac{1}{2}$ pint (1 cup) Dubonnet
$\frac{3}{4}$ pint (1$\frac{1}{2}$ cups) water
4 tablespoons icing
    (confectioners) sugar

$\frac{1}{2}$ teaspoon ground cinnamon
2 large eggs

Put the Dubonnet, water, 2 tablespoons icing sugar and
cinnamon into the fondue pan over low heat.
Meanwhile, whisk the egg whites until stiff, add the remaining
sugar and fold in the egg yolks.
When the Dubonnet is just below boiling point, pour into heat
proof goblets and top each with a good spoonful of the egg
mixture. Sprinkle each with a little cinnamon.
Serves 5-6

Claret and Orange Cup

*Your guests will appreciate this warming drink before they leave on a
cold evening.*

2$\frac{1}{2}$ pints (5 cups) claret
juice of 2 oranges
1 piece (1 inch) cinnamon
    stick
$\frac{1}{4}$ teaspoon ground cloves

$\frac{1}{4}$ teaspoon ground cinnamon
4 oz. (1 cup, lightly packed)
    brown sugar
2 oranges, washed, thinly
    sliced but not peeled, and
    pipped

All the ingredients can be ready in the bowl and the heat
applied when required. Serve it very hot, in goblets or
heat-proof glasses, but do not allow it to boil.
Serves 4-5

Note If you have young guests or wish to make the Claret Cup go a
little further, add 1 pint (2 cups) lemonade.

RECIPES FOR REFERENCE

Basic Pancake Batter

4 oz. (1 cup) all-purpose
   flour
2 teaspoons sugar
pinch of salt
1 tablespoon melted butter
   or corn oil

1 egg
1 egg yolk
$\frac{1}{2}$ pint (1 cup) milk or Marvel

Sift the flour, sugar and salt into a basin. Make a well in the middle, add the melted butter, whole egg and egg yolk. Add 2 tablespoons of the milk and stir until the mixture is quite smooth. Gradually add the rest of the milk beating thoroughly until bubbles form on the surface of the batter.
It should be the consistency of thick cream.
Leave to stand in a cold place as long as possible before using.

To make pancakes
Heat a little oil or lard in a heavy bottomed frying pan, run it round the sides of the pan and pour off any surplus. Pour in enough batter to cover the bottom of the pan very thinly and cook quickly until the under side is brown, then turn or toss and cook the other side. Turn out on to sugared paper.
If the pancakes are being made in advance, stack them with a piece of greaseproof paper between each and cover with a cloth. $\frac{1}{2}$ pint (1 cup) batter will make 10-12 medium sized pancakes. If they are to have a savoury filling, omit the sugar in the batter.

Basic Mayonnaise Sauce

2 egg yolks
$\frac{1}{2}$ teaspoon French mustard
$\frac{1}{2}$ teaspoon each of sugar and
  salt
pinch of white pepper

small pinch of cayenne pepper
few drops lemon juice
$\frac{1}{2}$ pint (1 cup) corn oil
2-3 tablespoons white wine
  vinegar

Put the yolks into a small bowl, add seasonings and lemon juice and work together for a few minutes using a wooden spoon. Add 2 tablespoons oil 2-3 drops at a time. The mixture should now be thick. Dilute with 2 teaspoons vinegar, then continue to add the oil carefully at first, then more quickly as the sauce thickens. Add a little more vinegar from time to time. When completed, the sauce should be thick enough to keep its shape. Adjust the seasoning. Finally, add 1 tablespoon boiling water.

Tartar Sauce Add 4 tablespoons chopped capers, 2 tablespoons chopped gherkins and 1 tablespoon chopped parsley to the basic mayonnaise.

Andalouse Sauce Add 4 tablespoons tomato paste and 4 tablespoons finely chopped pimento to the basic sauce.

Curry Sauce Add curry paste to taste.

Remoulade Sauce Add 2 tablespoons finely chopped dill pickle or gherkin, 2 teaspoons finely chopped capers, 1 teaspoon French mustard, 2 teaspoons finely chopped parsley, a dash of Tabasco and 2 tablespoons whipped cream to the basic mayonnaise.

Béarnaise Sauce

4 tablespoons white wine
  vinegar
6 peppercorns
$\frac{1}{2}$ bay leaf
1 sprig each of tarragon and
  chervil

2 egg yolks
2 oz. ($\frac{1}{2}$ stick) plus
  1 tablespoon extra butter
1 teaspoon each chopped
  tarragon and chervil

Put the vinegar, peppercorns, bay leaf, tarragon and chervil
sprigs into a small pan. Bring to the boil, then boil until the
quantity is reduced to 1 tablespoon.
Beat the egg yolks with the 1 tablespoon extra butter and a
pinch of salt. Put into a basin over a pan of hot water, or into
a double pan, stir until the mixture begins to thicken then add
the strained vinegar. Mix well and add the softened butter
a little at a time, stirring continuously with a wooden spoon
until all the butter is used up and the sauce has thickened.
Add the chopped tarragon and chervil and adjust the
seasoning.

Note There are several good quality brands of Béarnaise sauce on the
market if you have no time to make your own.

Garlic Bread

1 long crusty French loaf
2 oz. ($\frac{1}{4}$ cup) butter

2 cloves garlic
salt, pepper

Cut the bread into even slanting slices, not quite through.
Soften the butter, crush the garlic and work it into the butter
with salt and pepper.
Spread each slice of bread generously with the butter, then
re-shape the loaf.
Wrap in foil and bake for 10 minutes in a hot oven, Mark 7.
425°F. Reduce the heat to Mark 6. 400°F., open the foil and
return to the oven for about 5 minutes.

125

Crispy Herb Loaf

4 oz. ($\frac{1}{2}$ cup) butter
2 tablespoons mixed dried
  herbs

juice of $\frac{1}{4}$ lemon
black pepper
1 long French loaf

Cream the butter well with the herbs, lemon juice and pepper. Cut the bread into even slanting slices about $\frac{1}{2}$ inch thick but do not cut right through the loaf.

Spread each slice generously with the butter mixture and then re-shape the loaf. If there is any butter left, spread it over the top and sides.

Wrap the loaf in foil and bake for 10 minutes in a hot oven, Mark 7. 425°F. Reduce the heat a little, open the foil so that the bread will brown and crisp. Return to the oven for about 5 minutes. Serve hot.

Savoury Butters

To serve with steaks, hamburgers, etc.

Devilled Mustard Butter
Cream 4 oz. ($\frac{1}{2}$ cup) butter
  with –
2 teaspoons mixed mustard
$\frac{1}{2}$ teaspoon curry powder
1 tablespoon lemon juice
$\frac{1}{4}$ teaspoon finely grated
  lemon rind

Herb Butter
Cream 4 oz. ($\frac{1}{2}$ cup) butter
  with –
$\frac{1}{2}$ teaspoon chopped tarragon
1 tablespoon chopped chives
$\frac{1}{2}$ teaspoon rosemary

Chutney Butter
Cream 4 oz. ($\frac{1}{2}$ cup) butter
  with –
4 oz. (1 cup) smooth textured
  chutney e.g. apple or
  tomato
$\frac{1}{2}$ teaspoon lemon juice

Maitre D'Hôtel Butter
Cream 4 oz. (1 cup) butter
  with –
1 tablespoon chopped parsley
1 teaspoon lemon juice
salt, pepper
Chill before serving

Chinese Plum Sauce

2 oz. ($\frac{1}{4}$ cup) butter
1 small onion, peeled and
   finely chopped
$\frac{1}{2}$ lb. (1 cup) plum jam
2 tablespoons soy sauce

1 tablespoon white wine
   vinegar
$\frac{1}{2}$ teaspoon ground ginger
$\frac{1}{4}$ teaspoon dry mustard

Melt the butter in a pan, add the onion and sauté until
transparent and tender. Remove from the heat, stir in all the
other ingredients. Return to the heat and stir until the sauce
is smooth and hot.
Serve with Fish Fondue, (see page 34) or with pork or veal.

Rice Pilaf

2 oz. ($\frac{1}{4}$ cup) butter
1 tablespoon finely chopped
   onion
8 oz. ($1\frac{1}{3}$ cups) rice

salt, pepper
1 pint (2 cups) boiling
   consommé

Heat half the butter in a saucepan, add the onion and cook
until it begins to colour. Add the rice and seasoning and cook
for 1 minute stirring all the time so that the rice is well
impregnated with the butter.
Add the boiling consommé, cover and cook for 18 minutes.
Remove from the heat and add the remaining butter.
This is often served as an accompaniment to poultry and meat
dishes.

Sugar Syrup

1 lb. (2 cups) sugar

$\frac{1}{2}$ pint (1 cup) water

Put the sugar and water into a pan and heat slowly until the
sugar has dissolved.
Increase the heat and bring up to a temperature of 200-220°F.
When cool, this syrup can be bottled and used as required
for poaching fruit or for fruit cups etc.

INDEX